It's a Working Man's Town
Male Working Class Culture

Male working-class culture, Thomas Dunk argues, is two-pronged. Working-class men actively construct sets of meanings and values in opposition to what they see as the dominant culture. Their opposition, however, involves a celebration of immediate experience and "common sense" that limits its critical potential and makes it fertile ground for consumerism, sexism, and racism. Male working-class culture thus contains the seeds of both a radical response to social inequality and a defensive reaction against alternative social practices and ideas.

Dunk begins with a critical review of the principal theoretical problems relating to the study of working-class culture and consciousness and the classical responses to these problems. He then provides a detailed ethnographic analysis of "the Boys" – the male working-class group that is the subject of this study. Dunk's acquaintance with this group allowed him to use conversations from a series of weekend binges and lob-ball games to connect theory with experience.

It's a Working Man's Town demonstrates that the function and meaning of gender, ethnicity, popular leisure activities, and common-sense knowledge are intimately linked with the way an individual's experience is structured by class.

THOMAS W. DUNK is an assistant professor in the Department of Sociology and the Lakehead Centre for Northern Studies, Lakehead University.

It's a Working Man's Town

Male Working-Class Culture

T H O M A S   W .   D U N K

McGill-Queen's University Press
Montreal & Kingston • London • Buffalo

© McGill-Queen's University Press 1991
ISBN 0-7735-0861-9 (cloth)
ISBN 0-7735-1304-3 (paper)

Legal deposit fourth quarter 1991
Bibliothèque nationale du Québec

Printed in Canada on acid-free paper
First paperback edition 1994

This book has been published with the help of a grant
from the Social Science Federation of Canada, using
funds provided by the Social Sciences and Humanities
Research Council of Canada. Publication has also been
supported by Canada Council through its block grant
program.

Canadian Cataloguing in Publication Data

Dunk, Thomas W. (Thomas William)
  It's a working man's town

  Includes bibliographical references and index.
  ISBN 0-7735-0861-9 (bnd)
  ISBN 0-7735-1304-3 (pbk)

  1. Working class – Ontario – Thunder Bay – Case studies.
  I. Title.

  HN110.T58D86 1991   305.38'9622'0971312
  C91-090220-8

This book was typeset by Typo Litho Composition inc.
in 10/12 Baskerville.

For Pamela

Contents

Tables and Map

x   Tables and Map

MAP

Acknowledgments

I have accumulated debts to many people in the course of researching and writing this book. Without the friendship and honesty of the men I refer to as "the Boys," and the many other people who freely offered their opinion on many topics, this book would not exist. I am grateful to everyone who helped me in this regard.

The research this book is based on was undertaken for my doctoral dissertation. My perspective on the relationship between class, culture, and ideology developed through many exchanges and discussions with faculty and students in the Department of Anthropology at McGill University. I especially want to thank Jérôme Rousseau, Peter Gutkind, and Carmen Lambert, all of whom provided shrewd scholarly advice, intellectual stimulation, frank criticism, and moral support.

Many others have also read all or part of this manuscript at various stages of its development. Their incisive comments enabled me to improve it in many ways. In particular, I am indebted to Rebecca Dunk, Lee Drummond, Harvey Feit, Nancy Kramarich, Chris McAll, Lynn Phillips, Stuart Philpott (and the participants in his graduate seminar in the anthropology of work), Pamela Wakewich, Donald Wells, and the anonymous reviewers for McGill-Queen's University Press and the Social Science Federation of Canada. Of course, I alone am responsible for any errors or misinterpretations. I am also obliged to Claire Gigantes for her editorial skills, and to Peter Blaney and Joan McGilvray of McGill-Queen's University Press who guided me through the publication process.

I survived my graduate-student days thanks to the generous support of a McConnell Foundation Fellowship and a Social Sciences and Humanities Research Council of Canada Doctoral Fellowship. This book was produced with the financial help provided by a Social

Sciences and Humanities Research Council Post-Doctoral Research Fellowship and the office of the Dean of Arts and Science at Lakehead University.

Finally, to Pamela, Justine, and Maura, who have rearranged their lives so many times for me, I can only say thank you.

PART ONE

Introductions

CHAPTER ONE

Methodological Beginnings

AIM OF THE WORK

To question the ordinary, the routine, the everyday is a necessary project for a truly critical social science. The enduring importance of a work such as Barthes' *Mythologies* (1973) is that it brings the ordinary stuff of everyday life into a sharp focus and reveals how it is related to ideology and the exercise of power. Objects and practices normally taken for granted are shown to be social symbols with political significance.

This book describes and analyzes aspects of the culture of young white working-class men. Their culture is prosaic rather than poetic. It revolves around the local and immediate; it celebrates the ordinary, the profane – what is often referred to as mass culture. I show how this culture is intimately related to a sense of class, and how rejection of and resistance to a perceived dominant culture is expressed and deflected into non-class discourses. I focus specifically on leisure, gender, ethnicity, and regionalism, showing their relation to a preferred form of thought which is rooted in the local working-class experience.

My study is a contribution to the ongoing debate on the nature of the contemporary Western working class, and the relationship between domination and consent within the modern capitalist state. The book is an examination of the degree to which white working-class men are able to understand their own position in contemporary capitalist society, and of the limitations of this perception. To date, few anthropologists have taken part in this discussion. Practitioners of industrial anthropology have for the most part maintained a rather narrow focus on the labour process. They have not systematically addressed the broader issues of class and consciousness.[1] This is unfortunate because the debate revolves around an issue that has been the concern of anthropologists since the inception of the discipline, namely, the question of culture and its relation to economic, political, and ideological phenomena. Historians, sociologists, political scientists, and literary critics are engaged in an argument over the usefulness of the concept of culture and anthropological methods such as participant observation in the analysis of working-class life.

In the following pages, I argue that the celebration of the local, the ordinary, of mass culture by the white male working class in Thunder Bay is itself a form of class resistance to their subordination, but it is a reaction which inevitably entails strict limitations and is therefore easily diverted in other directions.

Discussing issues such as ethnic prejudice and sexism among the male working class can be hazardous because there is already a widespread image of the bigoted and authoritarian working man – an Archie Bunker, to refer to one of its popular incarnations – and one does not wish to contribute to this stereotype, which is itself an element of class prejudice. Many Marxist analyses ignore these phenomena among the working class and concentrate on beliefs and activities which conform to what some forms of Marxist theory assert correct class consciousness ought to be. But romantic images of the worker as the honest man, rough cut perhaps, but a "real person" struggling to maintain his dignity in a world that gives him no respect, or alternatively as an actual or potential revolutionary, politically involved, trying to preserve communal ideals against the onslaught of individuating and alienating structures of capitalism, can be just as obfuscating and politically hazardous as negative bourgeois images of the working class.

It is difficult to write about the working class without getting caught up in these competing representations of what the working class is really like. Let me start, then, with a couple of caveats. When I discuss, for instance, ethnic prejudice and sexism among the white male working class I am not suggesting that these individuals are more prejudiced than any other group in society. The argument is simply that these phenomena are an element in the culture of the working-class men I have studied and lived among and as such must be examined. They are discourses and practices with their own logic which exist throughout society. However, they have a specific meaning in working-class consciousness because of the class experience and the mode of thought which this experience generates. I am trying to avoid the pitfalls of romanticism on one side and intellectual snobbery on the other. The working class is neither essentially good, nor essentially bad; it is a complex social grouping which contains many positive features and some less admirable qualities.[2]

METHODOLOGY

Defining the Working Class

According to Wright (1976, 30–1), three economic criteria define the working class: lack of control over the physical means of production, over investments and the process of accumulation, and over other people's labour power. The working class is distinguished from the bourgeoisie in that the bourgeoisie does have control over these three phenomena – the physical means of production, investments and the process of accumulation, and other people's labour power.

The petty bourgeoisie is differentiated from the working class because it controls the physical means of production, investments, and the process of accumulation, but is like the proletariat in that it does not control other people's labour power. The petty bourgeoisie, therefore, shares certain features with both the working class and the bourgeoisie. However, the petty bourgeoisie is a class within the petty commodity mode of production, whereas the working class and the bourgeoisie are the two fundamental classes in the capitalist mode of production. Thus, the petty bourgeoisie is not to be understood as an intermediate class between the bourgeoisie and the working class in a tripartite hierarchy.

This definition of the working class is wider than others in which the working class includes only those workers who both produce surplus value and are engaged in "productive labour." According to Poulantzas, in the capitalist mode of production productive labour is "labour that produces surplus-value while *directly reproducing the material elements that serve as the substratum of the relation of exploitation: labour that is directly involved in material production by producing use-values that increase material wealth*" (Poulantzas 1978, 216; emphasis in original). The working class thus includes only industrial wage workers.

Marx's own definition of productive labour, from the viewpoint of the capitalist mode of production, is much wider. It emphasizes the nature of the social relation between worker and capitalist, rather than the material product of the labour process. Productive labour is any labour that valorizes capital. The specific nature of the material or non-material product of the labour process is irrelevant, as is illustrated by Marx's famous comparison of a sausage factory and a teaching factory.[3] What marks labour as productive from the viewpoint of capital is its ability to generate surplus value: "Since the immediate purpose and the *authentic product* of capitalist production is *surplus-value, labour is only productive*, and an exponent of labour-power is only a *productive worker*, if it or he creates *surplus-value* directly, i.e. the only productive labour is that which is directly *con-sumed* in the course of production for the valorization of capital" (Marx 1977, 1038; emphasis in original).

The broader definition of productive labour is important for understanding contemporary "post-industrial" capitalist society in Western Europe and North America. However much the labour process and products, and therefore the working class, have changed, the goal of the economy remains the production of surplus value. Whether that is to be achieved by producing hamburgers or ideas rather than steel or automobiles is of little concern to capital, as is whether the labour it exploits wears blue, white, or pink collars.

While economic criteria are crucial to the definition of class, they are not sufficient in themselves. Class formation and dissolution is an ongoing process which involves political and cultural factors, as well as relations of production. *"Classes are not given uniquely by any objective positions because they constitute effects of struggles, and these struggles are not determined uniquely by the relations of production"* (Przeworski 1986, 66; emphasis in original). The working class as a whole is centred upon individuals who occupy a proletarian position in the relations of production but it is not restricted to these individuals. In a given conjuncture it is possible that people who occupy contradictory class positions in the relations of production or who, like the petty bourgeoisie, are involved in a non-capitalist mode of production, may or may not adopt working-class positions in the class struggle, a struggle which is waged in terms of economics, politics, and culture. Contemporary capitalist societies (and industrialized socialist societies as well) include a high degree of specialization in the sphere of production, and this fragments classes. Cultural and political factors may exacerbate intra-class divisions rooted in objective economic differences or may contribute to the constitution of class-based identities despite these divisions.

The informal group from which much of the descriptive material in this book is drawn is composed of individuals involved in a variety of jobs. They are not all productive workers in Marx's sense of the term, nor do they all occupy unambiguous proletarian positions in the relations of production. The cultural world I describe in this book is centred upon people who are proletarian, but it is not limited to them. Indeed, my informants' idea that the city, where most of the fieldwork was carried out, is a "working man's town" illustrates their perception that working-class values colour the culture of the entire city, even though not all of its inhabitants are working class in a strictly economic sense.

The concept of "working class" is not a part of the everyday vocabulary of the people I studied, although they recognized its validity when I explained what I meant by the term. They describe themselves in several different ways depending upon the context. Sometimes they identify themselves as "middle class," thereby denoting their position in a tripartite hierarchy based on wealth. In this image of society there are three classes: the very rich, or the upper class; those, neither rich nor poor, who form the middle class (where they locate themselves); and the poor, who form the lower class. They also frequently speak in terms that indicate a dualistic conception of society. They refer to themselves as "the average man," or "the ordinary Joe," in opposition to "the big shots," or "important people." But their everyday language also contains words which reflect their place in the relations of production. Concepts such as "the working man," "the poor working stiff," "a hard hat," and "the lunch bucket brigade," which they apply to themselves, connote a certain kind of work experience – the types of clothes and equipment that are worn, how they feed themselves during the work day – which is perceived to be different from that of others.

The Informal Group

Anyone who wishes to conduct ethnographic research must find a way into the cultural world he or she plans to investigate. My way into the culture of the male working class was through an informal group of male friends. My research was not limited to this group, but over the two years I conducted my field research the twenty-one individuals who were the core of the informal group were my key informants. Participant observation was carried out mostly, but not only, with them.

The informal group is a central feature of male working-class culture. It can be understood as an opposition to the formal structures of school during childhood and work in adult life, but also to the bureaucracy in the modern state. The distinction between formal and informal is fundamental to working-class culture. "In working class culture generally opposition is frequently marked by a withdrawal into the informal and expressed in its characteristic mode just beyond the reach of 'the rule'" (Willis 1977, 22–3).

Within the workplace one of the ongoing struggles is to gain informal control of the labour process. "Systematic soldiering," "gold bricking," and the transformation of work into a game are well-documented techniques of informally resisting the intensity of exploitation in the labour process (Burawoy 1979b).[4] In the three years before I attended university, I worked in a paper mill, two different copper mines, and a grain elevator, and during high school I was employed with a cartage company and a feed mill. During this time,

I observed, and indeed participated in, the endless attempt to gain a measure of control over the job. Stretching coffee breaks, extra visits to the washroom, hiding in a part of the work site the foreman was unlikely to visit, working as slowly as possible ("fucking the dog" in local parlance), deliberately breaking thread and needles in the bagging room of the grain elevator, piling sacks of malt so they would fall over – all of these, and many other practices, were attempts to control the intensity of the work and to limit management's expectations of what could or should be accomplished in a given period of time. The basis of this kind of struggle is the informal group on the shopfloor. "It is the massive presence of this informal organisation which most decisively marks off shopfloor culture from middle class cultures of work" (Willis 1977, 54).

The informal group is also the basis of the joking and bantering that fill up a large portion of the work day. This social aspect of the job is where meaning and satisfaction are to be found, rather than in the work itself. "It's the people you work with that make a job enjoyable. As long as you got a good bunch of guys to work with, that's all that matters." This statement, by a retired worker, reflects an aspect of the working-class attitude towards work, and indicates how it is through the cultural practices of the informal group that an alienating situation is invested with meaning.

Informal groups exist outside the workplace as well, and any individual is likely to be involved in more than one. Next to the family, these informal groups are the most important social institution in the lives of many workers. They may overlap to a certain extent; because of their informality they tend to have fluid boundaries. There is a core of friends, perhaps, but not necessarily, from work, and then people who participate more or less intensely in group activities, and who are thus more or less marginal to the group. Moreover, the group is always in a state of flux. Membership is a matter of friendship and shared interests. As these wax and wane the individuals in any informal group change.

The informal group on which my study is centred existed outside of the workplace. I refer to the members of the group as "the Boys." Statements such as "hanging out with the boys," "being one of the boys," "he is one of the boys," "acting like one of the boys," are all local ways of referring to the phenomenon of the male informal group and the cultural practices which are related to it. Shared interest in certain leisure activities, especially sport and its attendant social practices, was the primary *raison d'être* of the group. It is difficult to put an exact number on the size of the group because the boundaries fluctuated, the group overlapped with others, and it

Table 1
Occupations of Twenty-One Key Informants Using Major and Minor Groups,
Statistics Canada 1971 Occupational Classifications

Artistic, Literary, Recreational, and Related Occupations	1
Clerical and Related Occupations	
Material Recording, Scheduling, and Distributing	4
Service Occupations	
Protective Service Occupations	2
Food and Beverage Preparation and Related Occupations	1
Processing Occupations	
Pulp and Papermaking and Related Occupations	5
Food, Beverage, and Related Processing Occupations	1
Construction Trades Occupations	4
Students	3

changed through time. My twenty-one key informants belonged to a variety of social networks, and they frequently brought other friends along to drink beer or play softball. In the bar after a softball game, for instance, the boundaries of the various informal groups become more malleable. Membership in one group makes one part of a larger community, an extended informal group.

The twenty-one individuals at the centre of this study were all, with one exception, between twenty-two and thirty years of age. As Table One shows, they were employed in several occupations, and three of them were students (two at university, one at a community college).

Much as been made of the divisions that exist within the working class, divisions between skilled and unskilled workers, between those in the "primary" and "secondary" labour markets, and between unionized and non-unionized workers, to mention only a few. These differences have effects on the experience of work, the cultural dispositions that are required, and the wages that are paid. Among my informants, such differences had not yet become personal and cultural boundaries. They were still bound together by an interest in the cultural world of young working-class men. Despite the variations in their occupations, the general experience of work was similar enough that it did not create divisions.

Some readers may presume that the reason for this is that the group was principally defined by its age, rather than the class position of the individuals. The men were, with one exception, all passing through young adulthood, a transitional phase of life between childhood and adulthood. It is the period when the pull of the male clique is strongest. Men in all social classes pass through this phase. But for each class the experience is somewhat different. For those of the "middle class" this phase usually involves attending university.

Two of the students in the informal group were at university. They, and other members of the informal group, originally met in high school. They attended university outside of Thunder Bay, and by the second year of my research no longer made an effort to keep up contacts with the Boys. Indeed, two of the Boys went to visit them in the city where they attended university, and returned from the trip furious with their former friends who apparently were too busy with their university friends to spend any time with the Boys. The visit marked the end of their connection to the group. A university education in this case helped form the class boundary. The other student was taking a technical program at the local community college. Age thus figures significantly in the description and analysis which follow, but how a stage of life is lived is inextricably bound up with one's class position. In this case, early adulthood was the time when social class began to divide childhood friends.

The various occupations of the Boys meant that their incomes varied significantly. The hourly rates of pay ranged from $5 an hour to $20 to $25 per hour. Such a range meant that the spending power of the Boys varied a great deal. In 1985, the average employment income in Thunder Bay for men who worked full time all year was $33,219, and for those who worked part time or only part of the year it was $16,156. Both figures are higher than the national and provincial averages. On the other hand, the male unemployment rate at 10.3 per cent was about four percentage points higher than the provincial average, although only slightly higher than the national average. Moreover, 45.7 per cent of all male workers in Thunder Bay worked either part time or part of the year, as compared to 36.9 per cent for the province of Ontario and 41.7 per cent for the country as a whole.[5]

In provincial and national terms, then, wages were relatively high for those who had full-time year-round employment, but in comparative terms the chance of being unemployed or of having only part-time or part-year employment was higher. Both unemployment and a lack of permanent, secure full-time work were problems for the Boys. Of the eighteen non-students among my key informants nine of them did not have full-time employment throughout the year. During my two years of field-work none of the construction tradespersons in the group worked for a full year. In fact, extended periods of unemployment were the norm, in one case to the point where unemployment benefits were exhausted. The work that was available usually involved short, intense stints on construction projects or upgrading schemes. Such work was often out of town and lasted from a couple of days to a couple of months. On paper the people with these jobs enjoyed the highest hourly wages, but they were rarely able to realize them. Climatic factors also had an impact on the availability of full-time work throughout the year. Several of the Boys were affected by seasonal changes in labour force requirements. Others were in positions where they were "on call," which meant that their work was intermittent. It could mean they did not know from one day to the next if they would be called in or not.

Thunder Bay has one of the highest rates of private home ownership in the nation. At the time of my study only four of the Boys had purchased houses. They all expected to do so one day, and they certainly considered it to be normal for one to "own" one's own home.[6] Seven of them still lived in their parent's house, while the others rented apartments.

Next to housing, the most expensive item of consumption for the Boys was their automobiles. Transportation is a problem in Thunder Bay and the region of northwestern Ontario as a whole. Within the city, public transportation is inefficient and automobiles are a necessity for most people who work there. Despite the fact that private transportation is a practical expenditure in this sense, it is also an important realm of cultural expression. One of the first things young men purchase when they leave school and begin work is an automobile. Possession of an automobile gives some independence of movement, and for those in their late teenage or early adult years, this is an important source of prestige. It is one of the chief attractions of entering the work force immediately after high school. Of course, the vehicle is frequently purchased with borrowed money, so that the mobility it confers is constrained in a larger sense by the commitment to work to pay off the loan. The purchase of an automobile is often the first step in the cycle that binds one into dependence on a regular paycheque. A popular bumpersticker reads, "I owe, I owe, it's off to work I go." There is more than a little truth in this for most of the working class, and perhaps for a large portion of other classes in modern society. For my informants this pattern begins with the purchase of a car or truck.

Knowledge about cars and trucks is an important element in masculine identity throughout society, and especially among young male workers. Seven of the Boys owned half-ton "pickup" trucks. These trucks had more symbolic than use value. They were not related to the work of the individuals. Two of the truck owners also owned cars. All the others but one owned North American cars.

Three of the Boys were married, five others lived with female partners, and four more were involved in serious relationships with women. Two of the Boys were divorced, and, along with the others who were single, were engaged in the search for female companionship on the one hand, while vigorously pronouncing on the freedom of being single, on the other. In fact, all these individuals were involved with several women over the two years of my research.

On Insider Research

The aims and inspiration of this study are at once personal and theoretical. The desire to undertake the project derives from my own life history as well as certain theoretical issues which are discussed in chapter 2. Rather than maintain the fiction that somehow the personal and theoretical can be separated, the two are interwined in the pages that follow.

My research, like all ethnographic research, was composed of interaction and dialogue between myself and the Boys (as well as others). The nature of that interaction and dialogue, or at least my interpretation of it, provided many clues about how the Boys think about the social world in which they live. I have made the nature of this process explicit by letting the Boys speak for themselves and by placing myself within the ethnographic description at various points in the text. Of course, this technique does not overcome all the problems related to the way ethnographic authority is created in texts written by anthropologists (Clifford 1988, 41–4). What follows is my representation of the interaction, and although in places the words are verbatim transcriptions of parts of conversations, I have chosen them to illustrate a certain point. Thus, the text is constructed according to my intentions and interests – I am not pretending otherwise. My aim is simply to provide some indication of the nature of the interaction (or at least my perception of the interaction) between myself and the Boys so that readers might better understand the experience that lies behind this book. The importance of explicitly addressing my relationship to the Boys and to my other informants is heightened by the fact that the research was carried out not just "at home" in the sense of my own society and culture, but "at home" where I was born and grew to young adulthood.

Anthropologists have been interested in their own cultures since the discipline began (Spindler and Spindler 1983, 49). Nonetheless, some anthropologists feel that research in one's own culture entails special methodological problems that are not encountered by those studying a foreign society. The perception of structures and patterns in one's own culture is thought to be inhibited because the researcher is too close to home: "too much is too familiar to be noticed or to arouse the curiosity essential to research" (Aguilar 1981, 16). Furthermore, it is suggested that insider research is inherently biased because the researcher is intimately involved in the culture he or she is studying (Aguilar 1981, 16).

In response to these claims, some argue that insider research is more effective than ethnographic research undertaken in a foreign culture because one's greater familiarity with the "home" culture makes it easier to recognize subtle but important differences, and generally simplifies the process of data collection. That the culture is lived by the researcher, rather than merely observed, is thought to enable a greater understanding in terms that are meaningful to the members of the culture under study. The shock of exposure to a radically different culture may actually impede research, and the outsider status of the researcher may render data collection more difficult and block the development of a subjective appreciation of the culture as it is lived. Moreover, the anthropologist working in an exotic setting brings the biases of his or her own culture and the analysis is inevitably ethnocentric to some extent (Aguilar 1981, 17–24).

Questions of bias and perception are significant issues for all social scientists. They are not solved simply by travelling to a foreign locale or by staying in familiar cultural surroundings. The argument about insider research, regardless of whether one is for or against it, is based upon the erroneous assumption that the anthropologists' own cultures are homogeneous and undifferentiated (Aguilar 1981, 25). Anthropologists, by virtue of being anthropologists, are always to some extent outside the group they are studying unless their subject of research is other anthropologists, and even then there are ethnic, gender, regional and intellectual differences that create boundaries. Inside and outside are, after all, relative concepts. The solutions to problems of perception and objectivity, in so far as they exist, are to be found in honesty, reflection, and criticism. It is not a matter of where one is, but how critically attuned one is to the structures and practices that generate and limit one's own place in a complex system of differences and similarities. The experience of culture shock may aid in the recognition of one's own cultural traditions, of the relativity of one's own culture, of what it is that "weighs like a nightmare on the brain of the living," to borrow a phrase Marx used in a different context (Marx 1978, 9), but it is no guarantee of this, or of observational clarity. From a methodological point of view there is no inherent advantage in doing research either at home or abroad.[7]

In this particular case, my personal experience was important in generating some of the basic questions this book is concerned with. My family background is working class. I quit high school after grade twelve without a university matriculation and went to work as an unskilled manual labourer. This decision had very little to do with a need for money. My family enjoyed a "normal," "comfortable" standard of living; in the terms of functionalist sociology we were middle class. Rather, my decision to leave school was related to the fact that I became part of a subculture in which "intellectual" pursuits, as they are defined by a Faculty of Arts at a university, are devalued. By the time I was in grade twelve I wanted to get a job "where one made good money," such as in a paper mill, grain elevator, or on the railroads. I wanted to have enough of my own money to buy my own things, a stereo, records, a car, to spend on the weekend, and perhaps to travel. Others might continue their education and go on to well-paid, comfortable, professional careers, but who wanted to be like them, the "suckholes"? So I was happy to get my first job in a feed mill; my father, through his work, knew the owner.

During the next three years, I had a number of jobs. I spent the summer in the feed mill. I was laid off in September. Almost immediately I was hired at a paper mill; the mother of a high-school friend worked in the office. I was laid off just before Christmas. By then I had saved enough money to finance a trip to Europe. When I came back in April I could not find a "good job" in the elevators or mills, and so I worked pumping gas at a tourist resort a hundred and twenty miles west of Thunder Bay. Luckily, within two weeks of starting this terribly low-paid and unprestigious work, I happened to have a high school acquaintance as a customer. He was working in the warehouse of a copper mine that was under construction a hundred kilometres further west. They needed people. Was I interested? After five months at the mine several of us had a chance to go to another copper mine in northern British Columbia near the Alaskan Panhandle. It was where "really good money" was made, and it was easy to save since you were only allowed out of the mine camp once every three or four months. Unfortunately, or perhaps fortunately, the price of copper fell in 1974, and after only four months I was laid off. So I returned to Thunder Bay and by April of 1975 I was employed at a local grain elevator; my father knew the superintendent.

By this time, the monotonous reality of unskilled work had made its impression upon me. I had also discovered that, even though I was part of "the gang," the informal group on the job, I was not very good at the kinds of joking and bantering with which people fill up the dead space of that kind of work. Indeed, in the track shed at the elevator that was what I was "known" for. The art of the quick repartee was beyond me.

It is difficult to recount why I decided to go to university. As with leaving high school, the decision was not the result of some process of career planning. As I remember it, I was simply looking for something to do because I was bored and so I enrolled as a mature part-time student at the local university. I took a course in anthropology at night while I was working at the grain elevator. In the spring I applied to a university in western Canada because I had a friend who had moved there. In the mid-1970s "everyone" was going west as a consequence of the oil boom. As it happened, I had some interesting professors, and only then did the idea of pursuing a career in the academic realm begin to develop.

The point of this autobiographical tale is that when I began to read ethnography and other kinds of anthropological writings I had a sense that there were often unstated and perhaps inaccurate assumptions about "our" culture which lay at the centre of these works. Like most of us I was not, and never will be, in any position to debate the facts presented in ethnographies of foreign cultures. I was not there; the writer was. But I had lived in "our" culture and it seemed that the differences between "us" and other cultures which were either implied or stated explicitly were not always as obvious to me as they were to the author, nor were the similarities. To put it another way, insofar as much anthropological writing is aimed at a specific audience that will, along with the writer, recognize the uniqueness of another people or the ways in which they resemble us, I felt left out. I did not feel part of the collective readership. I wondered just who the "us" was, never mind who the "them" might be. It was evident to me, if only in a vague manner, that the culture of the vast majority of the people at university, and especially those pursuing academic careers, was different from what I was used to. I had, for reasons I am still not sure of, left behind my working-class culture, but had not made the transition into the essentially bourgeois culture of the university. In this sense, I was an outsider and this marginality generated my interest in the subject of this book.

Practical Steps

I conducted ethnographic research in Thunder Bay, Ontario from June 1984 to August 1986. During this period I also visited the communities of Kenora, Dryden, and Fort Frances, all located in northwestern Ontario.

As I have said, my way into male working-class culture was through intensive participant observation with an informal group of working-class men. I also benefited from many discussions with older working-class men, and other relevant individuals such as government officials (municipal, provincial, and federal), and members of the local Native community. Library and archival research was carried out at the National Archives of Canada (NAC), Lakehead University and the Thunder Bay Historical Museum. I have also drawn heavily upon my own experience as a worker in Thunder Bay. Thus, while the image of male working-class culture in this book is coloured by the attitudes and practices of the informal group, the work is not solely a study of one such group.

Except for short family visits, I was away from the city for over eight years; however, initiating participant observation was relatively easy. Because of my own work experience in Thunder Bay I knew where the working-class bars were. I went to one that I had often attended and which is still very popular, and met some old friends and work mates. Through these initial contacts I was introduced to the various informal groups that regularly patronized the bar. During the first summer of my fieldwork, a form of softball was very popular in the city, and the bar frequented by my informants sponsored a league. I started going to some of the games and the weekend tournaments. That winter I played on a boot-hockey team that the informal group formed and the second summer I joined the lobball team.[8]

The bulk of my ethnographic data was recorded by writing out detailed descriptions of the events and conversations after they had taken place. I carried a small note pad and pencil all of the time in my shoulder sack and took as many notes during an event as was possible without changing the atmosphere. It is difficult in such a situation to try to record what is taking place without making the participants so uncomfortable that conversations or actions cease. I also taped formalized interviews with members of the informal group, and older workers whom I met through the group. However, I have not relied too heavily on these interviews in the description and analysis that follow. The formal interview is a particularly bourgeois way of communicating information.[9] The process was foreign to the way the men normally communicated with one another. Formalized questions elicited formalized answers. Responses often tended to be one word, yes or no, or extremely non-committal: "I don't know; it all depends how you look at it." This was very different from the conversations in informal settings, some of which are presented here, in which more substantial opinions were expressed on a variety of matters. Moreover, I am more interested in how the men express themselves within their own culture than in how they deal with artificial situations. In the context of the informal group, where the men are comfortable, themes of their own culture predominated, and conversation flowed more easily. In the one-on-one interview setting there was a lot of hesistancy in the Boys' responses. They were uncomfortable, no longer felt in control, and therefore became less communicative.

Furthermore, as Paul Willis notes:

Culture is not artifice and manners, the preserve of Sunday best, rainy afternoons and concert halls. It is the very material of our daily lives, the bricks and mortar of our most commonplace understandings, feelings and responses. We rely on cultural patterns and symbols for the minute, and unconscious, social reflexes that make us social and collective beings: we are therefore most *deeply* embedded in our culture when we are at our most natural and spontaneous ... As soon as we think, as soon as we see life as parts in a play, we are in a very important sense, already one step away from our real and living culture. (1979, 185–6, emphasis in original)

It is culture in this sense that I seek to untangle. I was therefore most interested in the Boys when they were at their most natural and spontaneous.

When I first began to hang around with the group I told them I was working on my Ph.D., which was going to be about regular working men and their attitudes about issues such as women and Natives. After a brief initial period of distance, during which I had to correct some mistaken views about students – a couple of the group members were convinced that all university students were paid a regular salary by the government, and that student loans did not have to be repaid – they were generally pleased that someone was interested in them.

But things were not always smooth. With time it became clear that many of their opinions were different from mine, and some of the Boys became rather defensive or in some contexts aggressive towards me. There were several incidents as well when individuals deliberately expressed very ardent racist opinions about the local Native community to goad me into responding. Overall, however, relations were good and most of the members of the informal group remain my friends. Pity and confusion are, perhaps, the most apt descriptions of their reaction to me. Many of them, once they learned what the financial situation of a graduate student in anthropology was like, could not understand why anyone would want that kind of life. From their perspective I had given up a well-paid and secure job for a very insecure future. Had I stayed at the grain elevator, I would have had more than ten years of seniority and a pension plan, and certainly would have been able to buy a house and a car.

The methodology I employ obviously imposes certain limitations. The informal group is a significant element of working-class culture, but it does not encompass the totality of it. I begin, however, with the assumption that any social formation is a structured totality, the elements of which are relatively autonomous, yet nonetheless related to one another.[10] A detailed description and interpretation of aspects of the culture of young working-class men will, therefore, yield insights into both the specificity of the practices and beliefs described, and into the relationships they have with other elements of the total system. Furthermore, culture is not a static thing around which boundaries can easily be drawn, or which can be faithfully represented by listing traits or characteristics. Culture is a constitutive, meaningful process. The aim here is to understand how it is constitutive and what meanings it has for the male working class through an analysis of specific activities and attitudes.

Studies of working-class culture have been male oriented. Indeed, families or couples are usually defined as working class in reference to the man's occupation. Marxist analyses have privileged production over reproduction, and therefore female domestic labour has been ignored (Luxton 1980, 13–16). The concentration on the male working class in this book is not to imply that the male experience is definitive of working-class culture as a whole. It is not intended to deny the significance of women as workers, both waged and unwaged, nor to suggest that women do not contribute at least fifty per cent of the totality of working-class culture. Obviously, there is a female domain of activity independent of men, and female opinions and attitudes are not necessarily the same as the men's. This book deals only with the *male* working class and, therefore, presents only half the story.[11]

The gender specificity of this study is itself a reflection of the salience of gender in working-class culture, and a sign that any simplistic attempt to discount gender in favour of class is bound to run aground on the rocks of reductionism. It was impossible to carry out intensive ethnographic research with women simply because there is a strong gender division within the working-class culture I investigated. Gender relations and stereotypes are changing (Livingstone and Luxton 1989), but patriarchal structures and ideology are still strong among the Boys. As discussed in chapter 4, the way masculinity is expressed and reproduced in the informal group is one of the factors which blunts the critical possibilities inherent in male working-class culture.

The informal group is also age related. It is frequently treated as a premarital phenomenon which loses any significance for men after the first year or so of marriage, although the "pull of the male clique" can present serious problems early in marriages (Komarovsky 1967, 28–32). The bulk of the ethnographic information presented here is derived from men in their twenties.

The process of aging obviously influences one's behaviour and attitudes. The wilder aspects of male culture decline in importance and life becomes more focused around the family and the home. One informant who was in his late thirties (he was not one of the Boys) had a cap which bore the following aphorism: "It used to be wine, women, and song. Now it's beer, the old lady, and TV." The general consensus was that this statement aptly characterized the essence of the transformation in lifestyle. But ideas do not change as easily. Attitudes about work, ethnic "others," gender, and knowledge are shared across the generations. Moreover, the form of practices may change, but their content may not be so easily modified. Male workers give up or reduce their participation in the life of the bar and the male informal group because they begin to initiate their own children into similar patterns. They leave the male clique of young adulthood only to join another male clique which meets on the sidelines of their son's hockey and baseball games. The patterns young boys learn in these games are the basis of their own future participation in the culture of young workers. Throughout this study I show how the culture of the Boys is specific to young male workers, but at the same time reflects or refracts cultural elements that are more widespread throughout society.

ORGANIZATION OF THE WORK

Chapter 2 contains a discussion of theories about the relationship between class, consciousness, and culture among the contemporary working class. I defend the idea that production relations are the most significant feature, although not the absolute determinant, of working-class consciousness, and that the particular meaning other discourses have is based on working-class experience of the process of production.

Chapter 3 presents a brief outline of the economic, political, and demographic features of the region of northwestern Ontario. The nature of work, the region's hinterland status within the province of Ontario, and the social and economic divisions within the region provide the context for the study of particular practices and attitudes.

Chapter 4 is a description and analysis of the Boys' interest in lobball. The game serves as a ritual text which illustrates important

themes in the way the Boys construct and express their own identity.
I argue that an intense interest in sport and an emphasis on having
fun is itself an inversion of the normal hierarchical relationship
between work and play in modern society. In this sense, it can be
read as a penetration of the dominant logic in modern capitalist
society. Much of the Boys' leisure style mocks notions of self-control,
discipline, fitness, and the work ethic, yet it is encapsulated within
a hegemonic culture based on consumption and gender.

Chapter 5 discusses ethnicity and ethnic prejudice through an
examination of the attitudes towards Natives, the largest visible minority in the region. Negative stereotypes about Indians have a long
heritage in European culture and this is reflected in the attitudes
discussed here.[12] However, local opinions about Indians and the
"Indian problem" are inextricably bound up with the role played by
common-sense thought, regionalism, and the welfare state in the
local white working-class culture. Attitudes about Indians are an
example of the influence of racism, but as a symbol Indians and
their perceived treatment by the Canadian state connote much more
than this. The Boys' statements about Indians are, at one and the
same time, statements about Native people and statements about
power relations among Euro-Canadians; they reflect an Indian/white
conflict and a "people" versus the "power bloc" conflict.

Chapter 6 examines common-sense thought and anti-intellectualism in white male working-class culture. I relate the importance of
these interconnected phenomena to the division between mental and
manual labour in contemporary capitalist society. The high validation given to common-sense as a mode of thought is an aspect of
the inversion of the mental/manual dichotomy in which the second
of these categories is more highly valued. This is an oppositional
practice which has the unfortunate effect of blunting the possibility
of more theoretical and critical ways of perceiving and thinking about
the social world; because of this, popular stereotypes regarding
women and Natives in particular become deeply entrenched.

CHAPTER TWO

Structure and Agency in Working-Class Culture

INTRODUCTION

In this chapter I present an overview of different theoretical approaches to the analysis of the relationship between the position of the working class in the relations of production, class consciousness, and working-class culture. I examine the classical Marxist position as formulated by Marx and Engels and the way this perspective was developed by a second generation of Marxist theoreticians including Lenin, Lukacs, and Gramsci. The last of these writers was the only one seriously to consider culture as an important element in the analysis of the political and ideological development of the Western working class.

A focus on working-class culture is the hallmark of recent analyses by a number of historians and is best exemplified by the work of E.P. Thompson. His writings on the English working class masterfully present the complex cultural processes involved in class formation, and in this way overcome the deterministic aspects of more orthodox paradigms. However, such an approach is marred by a tendency to cultural reductionism which may vitiate the usefulness of class as a concept.

I propose a theoretical perspective which avoids both economism and culturalism by maintaining an analytical distinction between the economic position of the working class and its cultural expression, and by recognizing the role of non-class discourses and practices in the formation of working-class culture. Thus, working-class culture is not viewed as a mere expression of economic interests, but rather as an articulation of various cultural phenomena in an oppositional struggle with the dominant culture which reflects the values and interests of the bourgeoisie. Lévi-Strauss's concept of the "bricoleur" and the Gramscian idea of hegemony enable us to understand the possibilities for the creation of new meaning using cultural elements from discourses and practices that are already established, and the limitations inherent in this process. They allow us to discern how working-class "penetrations" (Willis 1977) of the dominant ideology are so often mediated and deflected onto non-class terrain. The position of the working class in the relations of production does not determine the form of these cultural practices, but an appreciation of the dominance of a specific experience of work in the lives of working-class people is crucial to an understanding of the meaning with which these discourses and practices are invested.

THE CLASSICAL VIEW
OF WORKING-CLASS
CONSCIOUSNESS

The classical view of the working class in Marxist theory originates in works such as the *Communist Manifesto* (Marx and Engels 1968) and *The Condition of the English Working Class* (Engels 1969). The historical circumstances in which this paradigm was created left an indelible mark on it. The early texts of Marx and Engels which deal with the working class were based on their observations of the response of English workers to the new economic, social, and political conditions of proletarianization. This encouraged a speculative vision of what was to come, rather than a full understanding of the nature of the working class in a mature capitalist mode of production. The teleological bent of the theory is also a reflection of the domination of evolutionist ideas in the nineteenth century (Johnson 1979, 203).

The classical Marxist paradigm is centred on the distinction between class as an economic phenomenon (the class-in-itself) and a class conscious of itself as such (the class-for-itself). The concept of culture is absent. Popular or traditional beliefs and practices are at best ignored and at worst treated with disdain; their relationship to political practices and ideologies is not viewed as a concern. An intellectual élitism is evident, for example, in Engels's description of the pre-Chartist culture of small-scale craft workers: "They could rarely read and far more rarely write; went regularly to church, never talked politics, never conspired, never thought, delighted in physical exercises, listened with inherited reverence when the Bible was read, and were, in their unquestioning humility, exceedingly well-disposed towards the 'Superior' classes. But, intellectually, they were dead" (Engels 1969, 39). For Engels, class consciousness is expressed in the recognition by the class of its true political and economic interests and in the resulting struggle with capital.

As a class-in-itself the proletariat exists solely in terms of its position in the relations of production. It is a passive object brought into being and "thrown hither and thither" by the movements of capital (Johnson 1979, 203). This exclusively economic existence gives rise to the self-recognition of the proletariat which constitutes itself as a class-for-itself, conscious of its interests and struggling against capital. The end of this process is the negation of bourgeois society, the triumph of the proletarian revolution.

The teleological nature of this argument is obvious. A necessary and causative relation is drawn between the class and a specific class consciousness. Once the economic position of the labourer is established the transition to a revolutionary working class is preordained. The cause-and-effect relationship between a place in the relations of production and a specific form of consciousness is the root of the charge that Marxism treats culture as a mere epiphenomenon of the economic base.

Historical developments illuminated these fundamental flaws in the classical theory of the origin of working-class consciousness. A revolutionary working class has not been a major force in many capitalist countries. In England, after an initial period of extreme agitation and the early development of what seemed to be potentially revolutionary institutions, the working class settled into a process of coexistence with capital, of attempts to reform it rather than negate it (Nairn 1973, 188). Indeed, it has been argued that the more fully capitalism is developed in a given country, the more reformist the working class becomes (Mann 1973).

Much of the subsequent development of Marxist thought has been an attempt to account for the missing revolutionary working class. This was of primary concern to a second generation of Marxist theoreticians. Lenin argued that the development of class consciousness among the working class required strong leadership. Popular sentiments and beliefs were thought to be no basis for appropriate working-class political practice, and spontaneous agitation no substitute for a scientifically-based revolutionary strategy. Only a scientific analysis grounded in Marxist theory could indicate what the correct course of action would be. Even though Lenin was concerned with practical issues of political mobilization, he reduced ideological contents to their class character and insisted upon a strong division between ideology and the scientific analysis of a given situation. For Lenin, Marxism was science (Johnson 1979, 207–9).

Given the initial success of the Russian revolution, Lenin's theory of how to generate the correct class consciousness might seem to have been corroborated by historical fact. Outside of Russia, though, working-class revolution was not on the agenda, and a new theory of working-class consciousness had to be developed to explain the actual consciousness of workers.

This is the problem that Lukacs addresses in *History and Class Consciousness* (1971). The essence of the capitalist mode of production is seen in "the solution to the riddle of the commodity-*structure*" (Lukacs 1971, 83; emphasis in original). Commodity fetishism generates the reification of social relations as they appear rather than as they are. Social relations in a capitalist mode of production appear to be embodied in things – commodities – which operate under laws of nature, independent of human will, rather than as the product of intentional human practice. Social relations are reduced to relations between things, subject to forces external to human desire. Human beings are subjected to impersonal forces – the immutable laws of the market – over which they have no control. The ideological expression of the reification of social relations is the domination of scientific method in the social sciences.

There is something highly problematic in the fact that capitalist society is predisposed to harmonize with the scientific method ... when "science" maintains that the manner in which data immediately present themselves is an adequate foundation of scientific conceptualization and that the actual form of these data is the appropriate starting point for the formation of scientific concepts, it thereby takes its stand simply and dogmatically on the basis of capitalist society. It uncritically accepts the nature of the object as it is given and the laws of that society as the unalterable foundation of "science". (Lukacs 1971, 7)

When scientific knowledge is applied to society it is no more than a bourgeois ideology: "it must think of capitalism as being predestined to eternal survival by the eternal laws of nature and reason" (Lukacs 1971, 11).

For Lukacs, the functioning of capitalism gives rise to commodity fetishism; however, fundamental world views remain attached to each class. These do not comprise the actual consciousness of the class. Rather, they are the consciousness which can be ascribed to it on the basis of an understanding of the social totality: "By relating consciousness to the whole of society it becomes possible to infer the thoughts and feelings which men would have in a particular situation if they were able to assess both it and the interests arising from it in their impact on immediate action and on the whole structure of society. That is to say, it would be possible to infer the thoughts and feelings appropriate to their objective situation" (Lukacs 1971, 51). The ascribed consciousness of the proletariat is consciousness of itself as a class. This includes the recognition of itself as both the subject and object of history. Marxism is the ideology through which self-recognition is achieved, not because it is scientific – science is bourgeois ideology – but because Marxism represents the viewpoint of the totality (Lukacs 1971, 1–26). Because the proletariat is the most alienated class in capitalist society it is able to transcend the partial vision to which the bourgeoisie, by the nature of its position in the relations of production, is necessarily restricted. Unlike the bourgeoisie, the proletariat is not divided into individuals by the objective conditions of its existence, since production is increasingly socialized while appropriation remains private. Consciousness of itself as a class is synonymous with the struggles which will negate bourgeois society. "Thus the unity of theory and practice is only the reverse side of the social and historical position of the proletariat, simultaneously subject and object of its own knowledge. From its own point of view self-knowledge coincides with knowledge of the whole so that the proletariat is at one and the same time the subject and object of its own knowledge" (Lukacs 1971, 20).

Thus, Lukacs is primarily concerned with what the consciousness of the working class ought to be according to Marxist theory, rather than with the actual thoughts and practices of workers. Actual beliefs are either ignored or encapsulated in the catch-all notion of false consciousness.

We have, then, two different approaches to the questions of what correct working-class consciousness should be, why it is absent, and how it can be achieved. On the one hand, there is Lenin for whom science equals Marxism, and this in the hands of a strong working-class party will triumph over the false beliefs of the mass of working people. On the other hand, there is Lukacs, who believes that Marxism is not science but an ideology, which, however, corresponds to the imputed world view of the identical subject and object of history, namely, the working class. Despite their different views on science both Lenin and Lukacs hold a narrow vision of the political implications and possibilities of "the less overtly political elements of a culture" (Johnson 1979, 206). The classical view of working-class consciousness, then, eliminates from analysis that which does not adhere to a predetermined idea of what consciousness should be.

Of the second generation of Marxist theoreticians, Gramsci stands out because of his interest in the role of culture in the formation of social classes. His formulations are inconsistent and incomplete (Anderson 1976), but he recognized the importance of the "'spontaneous philosophy' which is proper to everybody" (Gramsci in Hoare and Smith 1971, 323), and the cultural elements in which it is expressed – language, common sense, popular religion, beliefs, superstitions and opinions. Awareness and criticism are to be built upon an understanding of popular conceptions of the world.

Gramsci's interest in culture was related to more directly political concerns. He recognized the difference in the way political power was exercised in the states of western Europe and Russia prior to the revolution of 1917 and the consequences of this for revolutionary political strategy. In Russia, the state dominated life to a far greater extent than it did in the West: "the state was everything, civil society was primordial and gelatinous." A "war of manoeuvre" was possible because by capturing the state through armed insurrection one gained control of the entire society. In the West, there was more of a balance between the state and civil society:[1] "there was a proper relation between State and civil society, and when the State trembled a sturdy structure of civil society was at once revealed. The State was only an outer ditch, behind which there stood a powerful system of fortresses and earthworks" (Gramsci in Hoare and Smith 1971, 238). Hence a "war of position" was required during which the cultural and ideological groundwork had to be prepared for the transformation to socialism. In the states of western Europe the consent of the subordinate classes was far more important than in Russia. Armed struggle in the absence of the appropriate cultural preparations was doomed to failure (Anderson 1976, 6–9).

Gramsci also appreciated the role of culture in the constitution of alliances among subordinate classes. He realized that the hegemony of the working class in an alliance with other classes could not be solely political, but had to involve moral and intellectual factors as well. According to Anderson, Gramsci "stressed more eloquently than any Russian Marxist before 1917 the *cultural* ascendancy which the hegemony of the proletariat over allied classes must bespeak" (1976, 17; emphasis in original). In the opinion of Laclau and Mouffe, the move from the political to the intellectual and moral plane was a decisive transition. It goes beyond an assertion of class-based identities which are joined politically, and establishes ideology, which for Laclau and Mouffe includes what I refer to as culture, as the terrain on which identity is established: "For whereas political leadership can be grounded upon a conjunctural coincidence of interests in which the participating sectors retain their separate identity, moral and intellectual leadership requires that an ensemble of 'ideas' and 'values' be shared by a number of sectors – or, to use our own terminology, that certain subject positions traverse a number of class sectors" (Laclau and Mouffe 1985, 66–7).

As I discuss below, significant problems arise if one privileges the ideological and cultural in the constitution of identities. For the moment, it suffices to recognize Gramsci's contribution to Marxist theory in generating a greater appreciation of the role of culture.

WORKING-CLASS CULTURE AND CONSCIOUSNESS

Gramsci's influence is evident in much recent writing on the working class. The attempt to avoid reductionism and teleology and to place the actual thoughts and practices of workers at centre stage characterizes the recent concern among social historians with the ethnographic description of working-class culture. E.P. Thompson is the central figure in the development of this perspective.

Thompson's work is based on his understanding of the concept of class, which, in turn, is rooted in the notion of agency. In explaining the title of his book *The Making of the English Working Class* (1968), he says: "*Making*, because it is a study in an active process, which owes as much to agency as to conditioning. The working class did not rise like the sun at an appointed time. It was present at its own making" (1968, 9; emphasis in original). Because it is an active process, class can only be analyzed over time. Class "is a historical phenomenon. I do not see class as a 'structure,' nor even as a 'category,' but as something which in fact happens (and can be shown to have happened) in human relationships" (Thompson 1968, 9). Class happens because of the common experiences of a group of people whose interests are different from and usually opposed to the interests of another group.

Thompson's vision of the relationship between the economic position of a class and its consciousness can be juxtaposed to that of the classical Marxist view. In Thompson's formulation, there is no determination of the specifics of class consciousness by the economic existence of class, no ascribed consciousness which a class ought to have if it is to be aware of its own interest.

The class experience is largely determined by the productive relations into which men are born – or enter involuntarily. Class-consciousness is the way in which these experiences are handled in cultural terms: embodied in traditions, value-systems, ideas and institutional forms. If the experience appears as determined, class-consciousness does not. We can see a *logic* in the responses of similar occupational groups undergoing similar experiences, but we cannot predict any law. Consciousness of class arises in the same way in different times and places, but never in just the same way. (Thompson 1968, 10; emphasis in original)

On this basis Thompson describes in great detail over some nine hundred pages the development of the culture of the English working class from 1792 to 1832. The depth of the empirical description is awe-inspiring. However, the book is hampered by the absence of theoretical generalizations regarding the issues he describes. Explanation is eschewed in favour of empirical description, but in the absence of more general principles there is little one can say about the material presented other than to recount various descriptive passages.

This problem is related to and exacerbated by a tendency to collapse the material/cultural distinction into the cultural. Thompson rejects the base/superstructure distinction upon which economistic Marxism and the classical view of the working class is based.

I am persuaded that I must abandon that curiously static concept, "basis" and "superstructure," which in a dominant Marxist tradition identifies basis with economies and affirms a heuristic priority to economic needs and behaviour over norms and value-systems. We may both assert "social being determines social consciousness" (an assertion which still calls for scrupulous examination and qualification) while leaving open for common investigation the question as to how far it is meaningful, in any given society, to describe "social being" independently of the norms, and primary cognitive structures, as well as material needs, around which existence is organized. (1978a, 261)

The preferred formulation of the relationship between economic structures and the other elements of a given social formation is taken from Marx's *Grundrisse*: "In all forms of society it is a determinate production and its relations which assign every other production and its relation their rank and influence. It is a general illumination in which all other colours are plunged and which modifies their specific tonalities. It is a special ether which defines the specific gravity of everything found in it" (cited in Thompson 1978a, 261). Rather than a distinction between base and superstructure we have a social totality, every element of which expresses the determinate form of production. But the determinate form of production is also embodied in culturally-determinate norms and ideas.

Anthropologists, including Marxist anthropologists, have long insisted upon the impossibility of describing the economy of primitive societies indepen-

dently of the kinship systems according to which these are structured, and
the kinship obligations and reciprocities which are as much endorsed and
enforced by norms as by needs. But it is equally true that in more advanced
societies the same distinctions are invalid ... There is no way in which I find
it possible to describe the Puritan or Methodist work discipline as an element
of the "superstructure" and then put work itself in a "basis" somewhere else.
(Thompson 1978a, 262)

These theoretical insights mark progress over the economic reductionism characteristic of the classic view of the proletariat. However, they entail certain problems, especially with regard to the
analysis of working-class culture; namely, how do we define what is
specifically working-class culture, if we do not initially identify the
class on the basis of its position in the relations of production?

The subject of much of Thompson's *The Making of the English
Working Class* is not the working class but artisans and petty commodity producers who are in the process of being proletarianized.
The radical culture he describes is the culture of people who are in
the process of losing the status, prestige, and way of life to which
they have become accustomed. Their radicalism is rooted in the fact
that the norms and values by which they lived are no longer relevant
in the economic conditions which are being established. After the
period described by Thompson the political culture of the English
working class changed significantly, becoming more reform oriented
than revolutionary or even radical (Nairn 1973). The Chartist movement expressed its aims in a language that was not specifically working class. It did not orient its criticism of the system to the nature
of production relations but to the nature of political representation
in the state and the issue of universal suffrage (Stedman Jones 1983).

The problem becomes one of defining which set of cultural forms
and contents represents the real working class. If the class is defined
in cultural terms only, it is very difficult to specify what, if anything,
is specifically working class about the myriad of cultural forms and
practices of the people who occupy the place of the proletariat in
the relations of production.

The practical tendency of the culturalist paradigm to collapse class
into a cultural formation may eliminate class struggle from consid-
eration, or generate an over-extension of the notion of struggle such
that it comes to include all manner of beliefs and practices. Leach
(1967), for example, proposes a "degenerate culture group view" of
class. The primary feature of a class is that it is endogamous, to a
degree, and therefore exists as an independent subcultural group.
Each class is defined by its accent, educational background, leisure
practices, clothing style, and so on. Classes are maintained by the

fact that people tend to marry within the group they share these cultural characteristics with. Styles of speech, dress, eating, housing, and leisure are very important subcultural markers (see Bourdieu 1984, Clarke 1976, Hebdige 1979). They comprise what McAll (1990, 138–49) refers to as the "ethnicity of class." Leach does not, however, address the structural basis of these cultural practices. They do not exist apart from the common experience which generates the impulse for groups of people to mark themselves off from others. The maintenance of subcultural boundaries is intertwined with conflicts over the production and distribution of economic and cultural capital, and the social relations of production determine what role different people play in production and what portion of the product they receive. They do, therefore, underpin the system of cultural differences to which Leach attaches such importance.

Examples of the tendency to inflate the notion of class struggle may be found in Bryan Palmer's *A Culture in Conflict (1979)*, a study of skilled workers in Hamilton, Ontario between 1860 and 1914. Palmer makes an important contribution to our understanding of the political significance of many seemingly mundane elements of everyday culture. He also illustrates how traditional mechanisms of community control were used to foster class solidarity and protest. However, Palmer is not critical enough of practices which have their roots in sexism and racism. The charivari, for example, was traditionally used to "expose sexual offenders, cuckolded husbands, wife and husband beaters, unwed mothers, and partners in unnatural marriage, to the collective wrath of the community" (Palmer 1979, 63). Palmer (1979, 65–6) does have one example of the charivari being used against a strike-breaker, but otherwise from his own account it seemed to be primarily a means of enforcing community moral standards. As the charivari declined in the 1890s, its traditional function was fulfilled by an organization known as the White Caps, "a movement dedicated to the protection of maidenly virtue and wifely chastity" (Palmer 1979, 68). The White Caps were "obviously patterned after the southern vigilante groups attempting to preserve white hegemony in the aftermath of black emancipation" (Palmer 1979, 66). Working-class people may have comprised the bulk of the membership of the charivari crowd and groups like the White Caps, and sometimes these practices and organizations may have been used to defend class interests. But their role in the maintenance of racial and gender domination raises the issue of why class interests were defended in this way, rather than through activities and organizations which were designed explicitly for class purposes. The importance in working-class culture of activities such as the charivari and groups such as the White Caps draw attention to the significance of non-class discourses in this culture. They illustrate the way class interests may be overdetermined by non-class issues, or refracted through racist and sexist discourses and therefore misdirected. One must beware of falling into a "romantic abasement before every manifestation of 'resistance,' however exotic, peripheral, displaced or contained" (Johnson 1979, 224).

The problems involved in an overly culturalistic approach to the working class are especially acute when one turns to the contemporary working class. Not only has the classical culture of the proletariat disappeared but the industrial working class has decreased as a percentage of the whole as previously non-capitalist forms of production have been commoditized. Writers concerned solely with the culture of the working class in Britain, for example, see the disappearance of the local pub, of extended-family dwellings, styles of dress, traditional working-class songs, and so on as indicative of the disappearance of the class. In Hoggart's (1957) perception, the distinctive working class is disappearing into the drabness of an alien mass culture which is marketed by appealing to the basest features of working-class culture. Young and Willmott's *Family and Kinship in East London* (1962) is a variation on this theme. It is a poignant description of the destruction of a working-class community and way of life by the creation of a new housing estate. This approach has the merit of vividly portraying a moment of transition in the existence of the working class, but the class has not disappeared; it has simply changed.

The idea that there is no longer a working class, that everyone is middle class today, follows, in part, from an over-emphasis on cultural definitions of class. In the debate about the embourgeoisement of the working class it was assumed that the growing material affluence of workers meant that cultural values would more closely resemble those of the wealthier classes in society. Ownership of a car, a house, and a colour television was thought to indicate cultural convergence with social classes which had at one time been the privileged owners of luxury goods. But objects do not have a fixed meaning which remains the same in each context. Similar objects in different social contexts can have very different values and meanings (Clarke 1979, 242). The basic lesson of structuralist linguistics is that meaning is generated by the relationships between elements in a signifying system, not by the elements in and of themselves. Thus, while the increased material wealth of the post-war working class and the commodities which working-class individuals can now purchase obviously have important effects on the cultural form in which individuals live their class experience, they by no means necessarily indicate that the working class has merged into the so-called middle class.

STRUCTURE VERSUS AGENCY

We are faced, then, with a dilemma. On the one hand, there is a theory of class consciousness which is based on a rigorous analysis of the economic position of the class and infers from this what the appropriate class consciousness ought to be. Unfortunately, the actual consciousness of the class has rarely conformed to such theoretical prescriptions.

On the other hand, we have an approach which emphasizes the actual consciousness of workers and attempts to elucidate how class consciousness is expressed in working-class culture. This paradigm avoids the teleology and economic reductionism involved in the classic theory of the proletariat. However, it often results in an overly culturalistic view of class, which tends uncritically to read class consciousness and resistance into all manner of thoughts and practices. It also leads to a conundrum regarding the definition of the class. If it is defined primarily in cultural terms one must first define what cultural phenomena are specifically working class. What criteria can be chosen? And how does one deal with cultural change?

The problem is to find an approach which neither imputes a correct working-class consciousness derived from the objective structures of its position in the relations of production, nor ignores the determinative features of the economic position of the class.

The first step is to rethink the base/superstructure (or infrastructure/superstructure) dichotomy. This is an unfortunate metaphor with its connotation of a top and a bottom, and the suggestion of superstructure as mere icing on the infrastructural cake. But one must be careful not to throw the baby out with the bath water in the effort to avoid some of the pitfalls of this mode of expression. It is necessary to maintain the possibility of *analytical* distinctions without forgetting that life is not experienced in this manner, just as sunlight is seldom experienced as the different wave lengths of which it consists. It is possible to specify the actual components of our experience without confusing the analysis with the experience.

Godelier (1978) has attempted to maintain the base/superstructure construct and, at the same time, acknowledge the fact that superstructural phenomena such as kinship, religion, and politics are often the basis for certain social forms of production. His solution is to think of base and superstructure in terms of function rather than institutions or levels of society. Thus, insofar as kinship is the idiom in which relations of production are expressed it is part of the infrastructure, but this does not mean it is not also superstructural at the same time. "The distinction between infrastructure and superstructure is not a distinction between institutions, but a *distinction between different functions within a single institution*" (Godelier 1978, 764; emphasis in original).

Godelier argues that the *idéel* and material similarly can be separated analytically, but not in actuality: "All social relations *arise and exist simultaneously both in thought and outside of it* ... all social relations contain, from the outset, an *idéel* element which is not an a posteriori reflection of it, but a condition for its emergence and ultimately an essential component. The *idéel* element exists not only in the form of the content of consciousness, but in the form of all those aspects of social relations that make them relations of signification and make their *meaning* or *meanings* manifest" (Godelier 1978, 766; emphasis in original).

The second step is to consider the relationship between human agency and the structures which determine or limit the possibilities of intentional action. The notion of human agency is crucial if one is to avoid reductionism, and if change is to be explained in other than mechanical terms. However, one must keep Marx's famous dictum in mind: "Men make their own history, but they do not make it just as they please; they do not make it under circumstances chosen by themselves, but under given circumstances directly encountered and inherited from the past" (Marx 1978, 9). Human agency acts within and upon structures which exist independently of the will of individuals, but a denial of intentional human practice inevitably results in a collapse into a static vision of society, or into a view of social, political and cultural change as a simple reflection of non-human processes. To say that intentionality is a basis of human action is not to imply that consciously-made decisions necessarily lead to the intended results. But even unintended results, which are the objective structures upon which further acts are performed, are nonetheless the product of intentional human practice. Thus, we have to find a middle ground between absolute freedom and absolute determinism.

The problem with an overly structural theory of consciousness is evident in the Althusserian theory of the relationship between ideology and the subject[2]: "In truth, ideology has very little to do with 'consciousness,' even supposing this term to have an unambiguous meaning. It is profoundly *unconscious* ... Ideology is indeed a system of representations, but in the majority of cases these representations have nothing to do with 'consciousness': they are usually images and occasionally concepts but it is above all as *structures* that they impose on the vast majority of men, not via their consciousness" (Althusser 1977, 233; emphasis in original). This "unconscious" structure permeates society; it is a medium or fabric from which men cannot be extricated, for it is the way we live: "Men live their actions ... in ideology, ... *by and through ideology*" (Althusser 1977, 233; emphasis in original).

The ideological instance functions to provide social cohesion. Ideology supplies a "representation of the world whose imaginary distortion depends on their [individuals who live in ideology] imaginary relation to their conditions of existence" (Althusser 1971, 166). In the abstract, this is achieved through the process of "interpellation". Ideology presents itself in the form of a "Subject" which "hails" an individual, calls the individual out of the crowd, and therewith the individual recognizes himself or herself as a "subject" in regard to the "Subject." With this act the individual is subsumed under the "Subject." This supplies a datum for the mutual recognition of the "subject" and "Subject," the subjects' recognition of each other, and of themselves. Finally, it ensures that "everything really is so, and that on condition that the subjects recognize what they are and behave accordingly, everything will be all right: Amen – 'So be it'" (Althusser 1971, 181; emphasis in original). In other words, this is how subjectivity is created, a subjectivity which accepts the given as natural and immutable. In concrete terms, this is accomplished through ideological state apparatuses, the dominant one in contemporary capitalist society being the education system.

Althusser's formulation is an attempt to understand how social formations reproduce themselves, to explain why the multiplicity of individual actions produces a self-sustaining system. But his theory is too functionalistic. If ideology creates "subjects" out of individuals, and the state apparatuses which control this process are in the control of the dominant class, then class struggle is ruled out. The process of the insertion of subjects into their positions in the relations of production becomes a mechanical function of objective structures. If "subjects" are merely the creation of structures controlled by the dominant class, how can they struggle against them? How can they change them? Where do oppositional and alternative ideas, discourses, strategies, and practices come from?

Indeed, the ontological status of the structures which impose themselves on individuals is itself a problem in the Althusserian scheme. If they are not a product of human action, if they "precede" human practice, then Althusser's entire theoretical edifice resolves into idealism.

However, if one accepts the centrality of human agency in the creation of class consciousness, one must immediately qualify what is meant by the term. It is one thing to decide consciously to mow the lawn and to go and do it. It is something else again to decide to create a new society and realize this end. There is a world of difference between intending to do something and realizing the intention. Moreover, there are always unintended consequences of intentional actions.

Lévi-Strauss's notion of the "bricoleur" is useful in achieving an understanding of how intentional acts are shaped and limited by structures which already exist. The "bricoleur" creates new meanings by rearranging elements which already exist: "It is always earlier ends which are called upon to play the part of means: the signified changes into the signifying and vice versa" (Lévi-Strauss 1966, 21). The elements, or tools, available to the bricoleur are always limited. New situations must be handled on the basis of what already exists and this has important consequences: "The elements which the 'bricoleur' collects and uses are 'preconstrained' like the constitutive units of myth, the possible combinations of which are restricted by the fact that they are drawn from the language where they already possess a sense which sets a limit on their freedom of manoeuvre" (Lévi-Strauss 1966, 19).

But this does not prevent new meanings from being created – meanings which become one of the elements which can be drawn upon and rearranged in another context so as to produce yet other meanings. The contexts change to a certain extent independent of the meanings given to them. Thus, without eliminating the intentional, conscious human subject, it is possible to infer real constraints upon his or her freedom of action in the cultural sphere while maintaining an autonomy between the "objective" material situation and the cultural ways in which the experience of this situation is handled.[3]

The concept of hegemony is very important in this context. It is not closed in the sense that ideology is for Althusser. Hegemony is a process which has continually to be renewed and which is continually resisted and altered by the subordinate classes in society. But the ability of the subordinate classes to resist is limited because of inequalities in the means of expression. The working-class cultural bricoleur has to work with materials which are to a large extent given by the dominant class. The range of possible alternative and oppositional meanings is, therefore, constrained (Williams 1977, 108–14).[4]

THE SPECIFICITY OF CULTURE AND ITS RELATIONSHIP TO CLASS CONSCIOUSNESS

I have been arguing that it is possible to identify social classes analytically in terms of their position within the relations of production, but that this does not imply any specific forms with regard to the cultural expression of this material social existence. This does not mean that relationships cannot be established between specific representational forms and specific classes. However, the relationships are not cause and effect. We must not confuse "the general problem of *class determination* of political and ideological superstructures, and the *forms of existence* of classes at the level of super-structures. Note that these are two distinct problems: to assert class determination of superstructures does not mean establishing the *form* in which this determination is exercised" (Laclau 1979, 158; emphasis in original). Cultural or ideological elements do not all have a specific class affiliation even though classes do have objective interests.[5] The working class does have an objective interest *vis-à-vis* capital, but it is erroneous to assume that Marxism or any other formalized world view is the necessary or correct form of expression of this interest. It will be expressed in terms of concepts, ideas, morals, and ethics which already exist, but which can be reworked so as to be meaningful in a new situation. Often the expression of difference and opposition involves metaphor, and thus allows for the possibility of play between the idea to be signified and the signifier. In certain contexts, therefore, there is a degree of ambiguity in the expression of class experience. With regard to politics, more than one class may employ similar symbols in the expression of its class interest and experience at the same time, making class alliances behind similar symbols possible, even though the symbols do not have exactly the same meaning for the various classes.

The only way of conceiving the presence of classes at the cultural level is in terms of the form in which class discourses are constructed. The oppositional aspect of class relations has no necessary form of expression. "The class character of an ideological discourse is revealed in what we would call its *specific articulating principle*" (Laclau 1979, 160; emphasis in original). Laclau illustrates this through an analysis of populist political discourse. Populism has no class connotation in and of itself. Its class character can be established only by analyzing the way it articulates ideological elements in a given context. Nationalism, for example, has been linked to different ideological elements by different classes. In Germany under Bismarck the landed aristocracy linked nationalism to the maintenance of a traditional hierarchical-authoritarian system. In France, the bourgeoisie connected nationalism to the growth of the centralized nation-state in their struggle with the particularist interests of feudalism, and employed it as a means of neutralizing class conflicts. Mao attacked the bourgeoisie for its betrayal of the nationalist cause and related nationalism to socialism. In none of these examples does nationalism refer to a clearly defined essence. Only through analysis can the nature of the differences be established.

Is it the case that nationalism refers to such diverse contents that it is not possible to find a common element of meaning in them all? Or rather is it that certain common nuclei of meaning are connotatively linked to diverse ideological-articulatory domains? If the first solution were accepted, we would have to conclude that ideological struggle as such is impossible, since classes can only compete at the ideological level if there exists a common framework of meaning shared by all forces in struggle. It is precisely this background of shared meanings that enables antagonistic discourses to establish their difference. The political discourses of various classes, for example, will consist of antagonistic efforts of articulation in which each class presents itself as the authentic representative of "the people", of "the national interest" and so on. If, therefore, the second solution – which we consider to be the correct answer – is accepted, it is necessary to conclude that *classes exist at the ideological and political level in a process of articulation and not of reduction* ...

Articulation requires, therefore, the existence of non-class contents – interpellations and contradictions – which constitute the raw material on which class ideological practices operate. (Laclau 1979, 160–1; emphasis in original)

One must consider what this means specifically for the analysis of working-class culture. Western Europe, particularly England, is the home of the world's first modern working class. The way of life, the institutions, the beliefs developed by working classes in other parts of the world are implicitly, if not explicitly, compared to the classic example.[6] In the analysis of the new working class in the developing regions of the world and the old working class in the so-called post-industrial nations any deviation from the paradigm constituted by the experience of the European working class is seen as evidence of the irrelevance of class in favour of notions such as tradition, tribalism, ethnicity, consumerism, embourgeoisement, and so on. But the practices and ideologies of the contemporary working class, wherever it is, cannot be measured against a European example considered to be paradigmatic. There is no necessary form of working-class ideology, politics, or culture.

A more fruitful approach to understanding the relationship between class, consciousness, and culture is to analyze the specific ways in which a myriad of elements are combined to have a significant meaning for people who occupy "the poles of antagonistic relations" but who "have no *necessary* form of existence at the ideological and political levels" (Laclau 1979, 159; emphasis in original). The fact that in many contexts traditional beliefs and forms of expression are important in ideological and political life cannot be immediately interpreted as the overriding force of "primordial sentiments" or as the domination of the "ideal" over the "material." It is an expression of the fact that people are born into conditions they did not themselves create. These conditions include production relations, and factors of the "superstructure" such as language, beliefs, and distinctions between knowledge and non-knowledge.

The forms of these latter phenomena are not determined by the relations of production; they are the cultural elements through which the relations of production are experienced and in which this experience is expressed: "The scientific study of ideologies presupposes precisely the study of this kind of transformation [i.e., how non-class cultural elements can express class contradictions] – which consists in a process of articulation and disarticulation of discourses – and of the *ideological terrain* which gives them meaning. But this process is unintelligible so long as ideological elements are pre-assigned to essential paradigms" (Laclau 1979, 157–8; emphasis in original).

THE POSSIBILITIES AND LIMITATIONS OF CLASS CONSCIOUSNESS

Viewing non-class cultural and ideological phenomena as possible vehicles of expression of class interests has allowed social scientists to understand certain phenomena which had previously been relegated to categories such as tribalism. Shivji's (1976) analysis of the way ethnicity symbolized class domination in Tanzania is an outstanding example of this. Ethnicity was the symbolic form in which classes were defined and the class struggle expressed (Rousseau

1978). One can expect that in social formations where non-economic factors play a predominant organizational role, that is, where institutions that are superstructural perform functions in the infrastructure, class struggles will be expressed in terms which are not explicitly economic (Saul 1979).

However, non-class discourses have a real autonomy, and while they may provide a form of expression of class conflict, they may also mask such conflict. There is no way of predicting the actual meaning of these phenomena before the analysis. One must examine how class and non-class discourses intersect. For while an individual is assigned a subject position on the basis of place in the relations of production, he or she also occupies other subject positions on the basis of race, ethnicity, nation, gender, region, and so on. Thus, in the case at hand, the subjects are working class; they are also male, white, citizens, taxpayers, northerners, fans, players, consumers, drivers, and a number of other things. Each of these subject positions can intersect with class in either negative or positive ways, or in both negative and positive ways. They may further the ability of individuals to perceive the actual conditions of their existence or they may limit it.

Willis (1977) employs the concepts of penetration[7] and limitation to describe the process by which class consciousness is expressed and developed or thwarted.

"Penetration" is meant to designate impulses within a cultural form towards the penetration of the conditions of existence of its members and their position within the social whole but in a way which is not centred, essentialist or individualist. "Limitation" is meant to designate those blocks, diversions and ideological effects which confuse and impede the full development and expression of these impulses. The rather clumsy but strictly accurate term, "partial penetration" is meant to designate the interaction of these two terms in a concrete culture.

Penetrations are not only crucially skewed and deprived of their independence, but also bound back finally to the structure they are uncovering in complex ways by internal and external limitations. There is ultimately a guilty and unrecognised – precisely a "partial" – relationship of these penetrations to that which they seem to be independent from, and see into. It is this specific combination of cultural "insight" and partiality which gives the mediated strength of personal validation and identity to individual behaviour which leads in the end to entrapment. There really is at some level a rational and potentially developmental basis for outcomes which appear to be completely irrational and regressive. It is, I would argue, only this contradictory, double articulation which allows a class society to exist in liberal and democratic forms: for an unfree condition to be entered freely. (Willis 1977, 119–20)

The ways in which white working-class men partially perceive the conditions of their own existence, and yet are limited by the forms in which their thought is expressed and the non-class ideologies to which this expression is linked, are precisely the subject of this book. I argue that while certain leisure activities, gender, ethnicity, regionalism, and common-sense thought are means of understanding and expressing their class position, they also inherently limit that understanding.

There is a recent debate over the question of whether the working class has an objective interest in perceiving the conditions of its own existence, and ultimately of overthrowing a capitalist system. The argument is primarily concerned with appropriate political strategies for socialists. The heart of the issue is the relationship between class and non-class discourses. In the past it was assumed by Marxists that the working class was the only social class with an objective interest in overthrowing capitalist relations of production. As I have shown this was the assumption of the classic view of the proletariat. According to Lukacs, the working class is the only class without a vested interest in believing the dominant ideology. Even the culturalist perspective assumes that the class position provides a common experience upon which the class makes itself, even though it does not predict what form class consciousness should take.

Recent writers (Gorz 1982; Laclau and Mouffe 1985) have argued that given the fragmentation and specialization of labour in contemporary capitalist social formations, and the divisions that exist because of this within the working class, it is a mistake to believe the proletariat has an objective interest *vis-à-vis* capital simply because of its place in the relations of production. Laclau and Mouffe go further and argue that to assume the proletariat has an objective interest *vis-à-vis* capital is a form of crude economism: "there is no logical connection whatsoever between positions in the relations of production and the mentality of the producers. The workers' resistance to certain forms of domination will depend upon the position they occupy within the ensemble of social relations, and not only those of production" (Laclau and Mouffe 1985, 84–5).

According to this interpretation it is through discourses that subject positions are constituted. Given that an individual is subject to a number of these at once, there is no central identity that can be imputed to social actors: "a fragmentation of positions exists *within* the social agents themselves, and ... these therefore lack an ultimate rational identity" (Laclau and Mouffe 1985, 84; emphasis in original).

I do not dispute the decentred nature of the subject or that there are subject positions which are not determined by production relations. However, Laclau and Mouffe deny production relations any influence in the determination of working-class subjectivity. The necessity of paid labour and the fear of losing it dominate the lives of working-class individuals. Even in Western capitalist nations, where the working class, or sections of it, enjoy high wages and some security of employment, their participation in many other subject positions – as homeowner, consumer, driver, fan – depends upon their continued participation as wage labourers in a production process over which they have no formal control. The fact that there is a vibrant shopfloor subculture of resistance to management control which does affect the extent to which management is able to determine the nature of the labour process does not prove that the technical and economic demands of the labour process, and production relations generally, do not massively influence working-class consciousness.[8] It may not necessarily generate a socialist or Marxist ideology, but it is an inescapable fact of life. While it is wrong to impute an entire correct world view to the working class as Lukacs attempted to do, it is reasonable to suggest there are certain interests that are related logically to the structural position of each particular class or class fraction. As Goldmann (1970, 126–7) argues, it is difficult to imagine that a large number of peasants who are small proprietors could ever be in favour of the nationalization of the means of production since this would entail the end of themselves as a class, or that a large percentage of the working class could be against all salary increases so as to stay abreast of rising prices.[9]

Even those subject positions such as ethnicity, race, and gender which exist independently of production relations at one level, in the sense that one is born into a gender, ethnic, or racial category, are interpreted and redefined in the light of the experience of wage labour. Indeed, these are social categories and are experienced and lived through human practice. For the working class, and perhaps not only for the working class, a large percentage of this practice occurs in a labour process. Definitions of manliness and femininity are inextricably bound up with work. This is not to argue that work generates gender categories, but that it is impossible to extricate gender definitions from labour processes, unless they are reduced to a strictly biological level. The same argument is true for race and even more so for ethnicity, which by definition is a cultural rather than a biological category. Livingstone and Luxton argue that class, gender, race, and ethnic relations are constituted in wage labour, households, and communities: "we conceive of a hierarchy of determination such that paid workplace production relations tend to constrain the autonomy of household activities more than vice versa, while communities extending from both household and paid workplace spheres take up residual and more discretionary parts of people's time and energies" (1989, 247).

Thus, the working-class perception of its own conditions of existence, and the limitations to that perception, are necessarily related to the experience of the relations of production. Many non-class discourses are influential, but work is a dominant if not absolutely determinant fact of working-class life. This fact may be difficult to grasp for those whose occupations allow some control over their own schedule. The existential experience of knowing that one's entire life is going to be spent in a job which is not intrinsically interesting or rewarding is not something that can be gained by students or researchers who enter working-class occupations temporarily either for money or research purposes. Intellectual understanding of exploitation is not the same as the actual experience. In the chapters that follow I will show how various non-class discourses are meaningful for white working-class men because the way they are lived is intrinsically bound up with the experience of a specific position in the relations of production.

PART TWO

The Regional Context

CHAPTER THREE

The Regional Setting

TD: What makes Thunder Bay different? How is it different from other cities?

One of the Boys: It's a working man's town. Everybody carries a lunch bucket here. That's what it's like in northwestern Ontario.

A PROVINCIAL HINTERLAND

Statistically speaking, the informant's response is not correct. As in most Western nations today, the largest percentage of the jobs in Thunder Bay are in the service sector of the economy. But the economic and cultural importance of industries based on resource extraction in the city and the region as a whole is reflected in the image of the working man with his metal lunch box. From the perspective of the male working class this is an area where men go to work in work clothes, work boots, and hard hats, and carry a lunch box.

Northern Ontario comprises ninety per cent of the province's land. With the exception of some portions along the southern margins of the Canadian Shield, the region is covered by forest, rock, swamp, and muskeg. The environment is not suitable for large-scale agriculture.

Northwestern Ontario is composed of the districts of Thunder Bay, Rainy River, and Kenora. Compared to the Yukon or the Northwest Territories the area is not very far north, and the city of Thunder Bay, which is located in the southern part of the region, is not readily distinguishable from many other mid-sized Canadian cities. But northwestern Ontario is a hinterland for the southern metropolitan region of Ontario and, just as the region is geographically

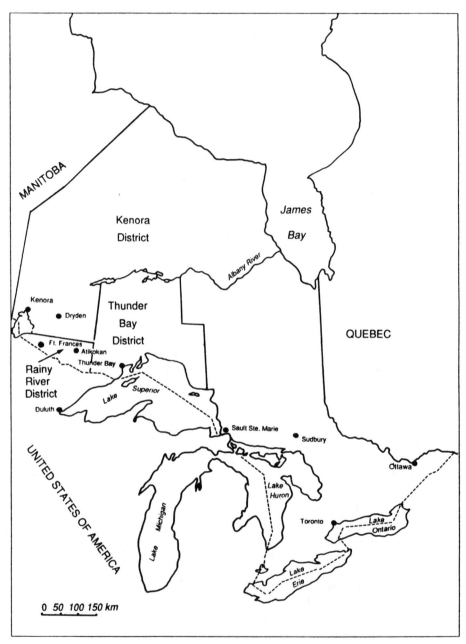

Map 1 Ontario – Selected Urban Centres and Northwest Districts

distinct from southern Ontario, so it is economically and socially distinct. These differences are exacerbated by the distance between the South and North. Northwestern Ontario is closer to Winnipeg than Toronto. The Trans-Canada Highway along the north shore of Lake Superior, which links northwestern Ontario to the rest of the province, was not completely paved until 1965. In many respects the region resembles the West rather than the East. From the perspective of Canada as a whole the region may not seem very far north and it may appear inaccurate to refer to the inhabitants as northerners, but within the provincial context the distinction between the North and South is significant.

Many Canadians perceive the province of Ontario as the industrial heartland of the nation. This image is perhaps accurate for the southern part of the province. In the North, however, the lack of secondary industry is striking. The regional economy is based on extractive industries such as forestry and mining, and on transportation and tourism. In terms of the number of people employed the service sector is very important in the local economy, but in terms of the value of the goods produced and wages paid the resource sector is the economic mainstay.

Because of its relatively narrow economic base and its heavy reliance upon extractive industries, northwestern Ontario is vulnerable to the boom-and-bust cycles typical of economies based upon the export of raw materials and semi-finished products. Throughout the 1980s, while the economy of the southern metropolitan region of Ontario was rapidly expanding, the economy of the city of Thunder Bay and northwestern Ontario as a whole was relatively stagnant. The economic disparity between northwestern Ontario and the southern part of the province contributes to the alienation from the South felt by many residents of the region (Miller 1980; Scott 1975; Weller 1977).

Northwestern Ontario has been a hinterland of the commercial empire based on the St. Lawrence River basin ever since the first French traders arrived in the region in the latter part of the seventeenth century. There is some disagreement about the distribution of Native people in the area at the time. Archaeologists feel that the present Native occupants of the region, the Cree and Ojibwa, are the ancestors of people who resided in northwestern Ontario for over seven thousand years (Dawson 1983). Ethnohistorians, on the other hand, are of the opinion that European settlement in the St. Lawrence River valley, the development of the fur trade, and the destruction of Huronia around 1650 had major repercussions on the distribution of Native populations throughout the eastern half of Canada. They believe that the Ojibwa are relatively recent arrivals in northwestern Ontario, moving into the region in the latter seventeenth and early eighteenth centuries in an attempt to maintain their middleman position in the fur trade, and displacing the Cree to the north and the Assiniboine and Sioux to the west (Bishop 1974; Hickerson 1970). In any event, the fur trade had a serious impact on groups such as the Ojibwa: "The documented history of the Ojibwa shows clearly their interdependent relationship with Europeans. From the seventeenth century on it would not be true to consider them as an aboriginal population. Perhaps because of their strategic location at the Sault rapids on the main western trade route and their early contact with Europeans they became thoroughly identified with the development of European interests" (Dunning 1959, 4).

The hinterland/metropolis relationship between northwestern Ontario and more southern centres was established with the initial European arrival in the area. It set the pattern whereby raw materials produced by the local inhabitants were shipped out of the region for processing and finished products were imported.

The famous fur traders and explorers Radisson and Groseilliers may have reached Thunder Bay as early as 1662. It is certain that Daniel Greysolon, Sieur du Lhut, constructed a small fort near the mouth of the Kaministikwia River in 1679 or 1680. This post was repaired by de Noyons in 1688. In 1717 Sieur de la Noue visited the region in his attempt to reach the Pacific Ocean. He built a new post across the river from the old Fort Caministigoyan.[1] La Vérendrye wintered on the Kaministikwia in 1731–32, after his men mutinied at the prospect of using a more difficult route along the Pigeon River, approximately sixty kilometres to the south, to get to the interior.

When the Northwest Company was formed in 1783, it employed the more southerly route to get to the West and Northwest, and established a fort at the mouth of the Pigeon River. The post, named Grand Portage after the nine-mile-long portage with which the canoe route begins, became the inland entrepôt of the company. During the summer rendezvous, furs from the interior were collected and shipped east, and supplies were distributed to the partners wintering inland. When the boundary dispute between the United States and Britain was finally resolved after the American Revolution, Grand Portage was found to be on American territory and was therefore moved north. The old Kaministikwia River route to the interior was reactivated and a new post was constructed at the river mouth around 1801. In 1807 it was officially named Fort William in honour of

William McGillivray, director of the Northwest Company. For a brief two decades it became a hive of social and economic activity each summer when company personnel from the interior met their eastern associates (Campbell 1980). When the Hudson's Bay Company and the Northwest Company merged in 1821, the post and the region of northwestern Ontario as a whole were relegated to secondary status as a source of furs and as a link in the transportation route to the interior. It was cheaper for the company to provision its inland trading posts through Hudson Bay. The pattern of boom and bust which still characterizes economic life in the region had begun. The Native population was the first to experience the effects of this cyclical pattern. Although one must take care not to overestimate the extent of Native dependence on European technology during the fur-trade era (Ray 1974), the decline of the fur trade in the region as well as disease and environmental change created a difficult situation for the Ojibwa and Cree in northwestern Ontario as early as the nineteenth century (Bishop 1974; Kue Young 1987). In the vicinity of Fort William fur traders frequently reported that the Natives were starving and that, as early as the 1820s, the land could no longer support them.

In 1841, the Ojibwa from the Thunder Bay area petitioned George Simpson, Governor of the Hudson's Bay Company, for land in the Kaministikwia River valley where they could settle and take up farming. He refused on the grounds that a settlement there was not in the interests of the fur trade. Simpson even took steps to encourage retired company personnel who had settled in the valley to move east to Sault Ste Marie (Williams 1973, 25–6). This is one of the earliest examples of the way powerful institutions located outside the region were able to determine the future of local residents.

The origins of the contemporary resource-based economy of northwestern Ontario go back to the late 1840s when the area's potential mineral wealth began to attract the attention of prospectors. The Ojibwa living in the vicinity of Lake Superior tried to compel white entrepreneurs to respect Native rights over the land and its resources (Chute 1986). In 1849 and 1850 they forced miners off locations at Mica Bay and Michipocoten Island (Chute 1986, 221–63). The government of Upper Canada responded by negotiating the Robinson-Superior Treaty with the Ojibwa living between Lake Superior and the height of land which forms the border between the arctic and Great Lakes watersheds. The region was conceived solely as a source of mineral wealth, and never as an area where there would be extensive white settlement. William Robinson, who negotiated the treaty, wrote to his superior of what he had told the

Indians: "The lands now ceded are notoriously barren and sterile, and will in all probability never be settled except in a few localities by mining companies; whose establishments among the Indians instead of being prejudicial would prove of great benefit as they would afford a market for any thing they may have to sell & bring provisions & stores of all kinds among them at reasonable prices" (Robinson n.d.).

In the 1860s silver mining became a major economic activity along the north shore of Lake Superior. The most spectacular discovery was on Silver Islet, a tiny rock outcrop one mile offshore from Thunder Cape, the tip of the peninsula that juts into Lake Superior to form Thunder Bay. Only after the Montreal Mining Company sold its interest to an American capitalist was the mine developed. Between 1869 and 1884, when a storm flooded the mine shafts, Silver Islet produced $3,250,000 worth of silver (Barr 1988; Blue 1896). But the history of Silver Islet also reflects the boom-and-bust cycle typical of the economy of northwestern Ontario. Little of the wealth taken from the mine stayed in the region and the town of Silver Islet, which had grown up on the mainland adjacent to the mine, died.[2]

Work on the Canadian Pacific Railroad commenced at the Town Plot, now part of the area known as Westfort in the southern half of Thunder Bay, in 1875. The railroad and the development of the port at the head of Lake Superior brought the first sustained economic development to the region. Construction of the eastern link to what was to become Thunder Bay was completed in 1885, but grain had been transhipped from train to boat in the port since 1883. The port remains a vital part of the city's economy. In terms of total tonnage it is the third busiest harbour in Canada, and it is the largest grain handling port in the world (Thunder Bay Economic Development Corporation[3] 1988, H-1). More than six thousand people, or almost ten per cent of the city's work force are employed in transportation and storage (TBEDC 1988, D-5).[4]

The forest products industry, which today is the mainstay of the economy of the entire region, only began to develop in the wake of the wider settlement which followed the construction of the railroad. Initially, it involved the production of lumber for construction, railroad ties, and pulp logs. In 1900, however, the Ontario government, under pressure from those with an interest in pulp mills, amended the Timber Act to prevent the export of raw logs. Spruce cut on Crown land had to be processed into pulp before it could be exported. American newspaper interests, concerned about the supply of cheap newsprint, lobbied the American government to allow

Canadian pulp and paper into the United States tariff-free (Easter-brook and Aitken 1980, 538–46; Nelles 1974, 48–107).

Northwestern Ontario was well supplied with spruce forests. In the then cities of Fort William and Port Arthur four mills, all of them still in existence today, were constructed in the 1920s. Since then the importance of the forest industry has grown throughout the region. A report by the Municipal Advisory Committee in 1977 stated that sixty to seventy per cent of northwestern Ontario's labour force was dependent upon the forest industry for its livelihood.[5] The industry directly employs over 15,000 people in northwestern Ontario. Forest sector companies in the city of Thunder Bay employ 6,500 people, about ten per cent of the total labour force of the city and surrounding area (TBEDC 1988, F-1,F-7–8). Pulp and paper and wood products comprise almost seventy-five per cent of manufacturing production in Thunder Bay, and pay almost eighty-four per cent of the total wages in the manufacturing sector (TBEDC 1988, G-1,G-3).

The pulp and paper companies are powerful institutions in northwestern Ontario. The four mills in Thunder Bay are owned by two companies: three by Abitibi-Price and the other by Canadian Pacific Forest Products Limited.[6] The latter also owns a mill in Dryden which it purchased from Reed Limited in 1979. Canadian Pacific Forest Products Limited is owned by Canadian Pacific Investments and Abitibi-Price belongs to Olympia-York Development of Toronto. In the early 1980s Great Lakes Forest Products (now Canadian Pacific Forest Products Limited) used its significant influence to stifle criticism of its forest management policies. The Lakehead Social Planning Council (LSPC), an independent organization which attempts to monitor the social effects of economic trends in Thunder Bay and the surrounding region, published a study of the forest industry in northwestern Ontario which suggested there was an imminent crisis in the forest industry due to a shortage of wood. The report attributed the problem to the harvesting techniques employed by the forest companies and the absence of a commitment to reforestation. The LSPC received funding from the United Way, a supposedly independent charitable organization, and the city of Thunder Bay. In response to the report, Great Lakes Forest Products and its employee charity groups demanded that their donations to the United Way be designated to particular groups, excluding the LSPC. The United Way cooperated with the demand. In 1984 Thunder Bay City Council also criticized LSPC because of the content of its report and reduced its funding. In 1985, the City cut its financial contributions to LSPC altogether. These decisions crippled LSPC, and effectively eliminated a local source of criticism of the policies and practices of the forest products industry and of the economic situation in the city and region generally. With the election of a new city council in 1986 some funding was restored, but it remains a hotly contested issue for the city council (*Chronicle-Journal* 14 April 1987, 15). In smaller towns where the pulp and paper mills play a proportionally larger economic role, the political influence is greater. Reed Limited, for example, was able to influence local media coverage of the mercury pollution of the English River system by its Dryden mill in the 1970s (Troyer 1977). This is further evidence of the hinterland/metropolis relationship which northwestern Ontario is locked into. Large corporations whose principal responsibilities lie with investors who live outside the region determine the economic future of the region and the lives of the local inhabitants.

There has been a very close relationship between big business and the government of Ontario since the 1930s. During the depression an "intimate personal and institutional relationship of government and business" developed such that the interests of the province became virtually indistinguishable from the interests of business (Nelles 1974, 487). "Algoma Steel, Great Lakes Paper, McIntyre-Porcupine Gold Mines, General Motors and Ontario Hydro largely determined the course of public policy; in some instances these organizations even wrote the letters and statements that appeared above the Premier's signature" (Nelles 1974, 487–8). In northwestern Ontario, where the narrow economic base enhances the power of the institutions of government and big business, it is difficult to resist their influence.

Weller (1977) has analyzed the political consequences of northwestern Ontario's status as a subprovincial hinterland. He divides the political response of the local inhabitants into three categories: the politics of extraction, the politics of frustration and the politics of parochialism.

The politics of extraction are characterized by a continual call from the region for a fundamental change in its hinterland status. This usually revolves around demands for expansion of the economic base of northwestern Ontario through the establishment of secondary industry in the region and for services that are taken for granted in other areas of the province, such as adequate roads and airport facilities. In terms of electoral politics the tactic of the inhabitants has frequently been to vote for the party in power at both the federal and provincial levels so as not to be left out of anything. The attempt to transform the basic relationship between northwestern Ontario and the rest of the province through such means has been and will, in Weller's opinion, continue to be futile. The region has only 2.5 per cent of the provincial population, and only five seats in the provincial legislature of one hundred and twenty-five seats, and four federal seats out of two hundred and sixty-four.

The response of the metropolis to local demands has been a "politics of handouts," which takes three basic forms: "The first is the delivery of what are seen by many local residents as bribes. The second is the delivery of essential services as if they were gifts. The third is the appointment of local figures to cabinet posts of relatively little importance" (Weller 1977, 743).

The politics of frustration is manifested in the strength of radicalism as an undercurrent in the political history of the region, and in fringe movements of various kinds which frequently appear. Radical ideas found a fertile breeding ground in the lumber and mining camps in the first half of the twentieth century. Many of these ideas were brought by immigrants from non-Anglo-Saxon areas of Europe. Finns were especially active in socialist and communist movements (Radforth 1987, 107–58). Factionalism and the concerted efforts of government and business in the region muted the effects of the radical current in politics but it is an important feature of local political history. "Few modern Canadian cities, with the exception of Winnipeg, have had a more radical political history during the First World War and Depression years. Equally few, Calgary and Vancouver perhaps excluded, have participated as broadly in the variety of political movements thrown up by the twentieth century" (Rasporich in Weller 1977, 747). Fringe movements have included attempts to establish a separatist party for the region and various environmentally-concerned groups.

The politics of parochialism involves both an inward-looking preoccupation with local events and conflicts and an internalization of the inferior status of the region. An example of the preoccupation with local conflicts is the rivalry that existed between Fort William and Port Arthur until their amalgamation in 1970, although even that did not completely end the squabbles. The competition between the two cities was often very petty – street cars on different time-tables, one city on Daylight Saving Time while the other was not – and it probably delayed some important developments for the two cities and the region. The politics of parochialism is also illustrated by what Weller calls "the almost pathological interest in local politics" (1977, 752). This tendency has been exacerbated by the concentration of local newspapers in the region in the hands of the Thompson chain which is conservative and emphasizes coverage of local "establishment groups."

The politics of parochialism has also involved the development of a dependency mentality in northwestern Ontario.

For most of its history much of northwestern Ontario has been run as a dependency of either the provincial government or large corporations. Those who ran the towns tended to be members of either a nonresident elite in Toronto or a resident elite which had been imported and was likely to remain only for a very short time. A politics of dependency thus developed with very few of the communities experiencing real self-government and with many residents developing the feeling that only those from outside the region had the requisite skills to govern or offer advice to the North. Thus northwestern Ontario failed to develop self-assurance in many matters which perhaps mirrored the general Canadian lack of assurance on the worth of many aspects of its own endeavours – until, of course, received favourably elsewhere. (Weller 1977, 752–3)

There is another aspect of the relationship between the dependent status of northwestern Ontario and the development or lack of development of self-assurance. In a reactive mode, local knowledge is celebrated to the point where critical self-reflection is ruled out. This is evident in the overwhelming importance local political events have for the residents. It extends well beyond politics in the formal sense of elections, however, and has important effects on thought generally.

I discuss this matter in detail in chapters 5 and 6. Although local definitions of what is important and what counts as useful knowledge are not determined by the economy in a simple fashion, the regional division of labour within the province of Ontario is an important element of the context within which regional and class consciousness mutually reinforce one another. The importance of practical common sense as a form of thought in local culture is intimately bound up with regionalism, and colours the way issues related to gender, ethnicity, and cultural activities are thought about. It is an important element in the "structure of feeling" that dominates the region.[7]

Regional occupational differences correspond in a general sense to a division between mental and manual labour, and therefore have a class connotation for the local working class. Employment opportunities involving invention, planning, and co-ordination tend to be concentrated in the southern metropolitan region, while jobs involved in executing the plans are located in hinterland regions such as northwestern Ontario.

The division emerges clearly if one compares northwestern Ontario with Ontario as a whole and with the city of Toronto. There are relatively fewer jobs in northwestern Ontario in management and administration, and in the technological, social scientific, religious, and artistic professions, than in the province as a whole and in the city of Toronto. The relative difference is greater if the city of Thunder Bay is excluded from the figures for northwestern Ontario. On the other hand, in northwestern Ontario there are relatively more people employed in the primary industries such as forestry, fishing, hunting and trapping, and mining, in processing industries (which include such things as sawmills and pulp and paper mills), and in construction and transportation. Again, the relative difference between northwestern Ontario and the province as a whole and the city of Toronto is more marked if one excludes Thunder Bay from the calculation. Another difference relevant to the present discussion is the relatively smaller number of people employed in clerical and related occupations in northwestern Ontario as compared to Ontario and Toronto, and the relatively larger number of people involved in the service occupations in northwestern Ontario.

Another way of stating this difference is that more than 60 per cent of the experienced labour force in Toronto is involved in some kind of "white collar" work, whereas the relative proportion for northwestern Ontario is 46 per cent (41 per cent if one excludes the city of Thunder Bay). "Blue collar occupations" constitute 32 per cent of the experienced labour force for Toronto and 48 per cent for northwestern Ontario (53 per cent excluding Thunder Bay). Given this marked difference, it is easy to understand why, for my informants, "mental labour" is associated with the South and manual labour with the North.[8]

Statistics cannot convey the cultural significance of the regional division of labour. Smoke stacks of the paper mills and the smoke which emanates from them, with its powerful and distinctive odour, dominate the skyline of Thunder Bay and towns such as Dryden, Kenora, and Fort Frances. On the major roads, trucks loaded with logs are the bane of regular commuters, and rounding a corner on a dirt road only to find yourself head-on with a loaded pulp truck is one of the more frightening experiences you can have. One of my most vivid boyhood memories is of a pulp truck which flipped over when its load shifted in front of my parents' home along the Trans-Canada Highway. The driver luckily escaped unhurt. These "facts of life" in the region are also important signifiers of the cultural difference between what the locals refer to as the North and the South.

Some aspects of the modern forest-products industry are descendants of the earlier timber trade. Workers in nineteenth-century staple industries are often romanticized.[9] They are celebrated for

Table 2
Occupational Profile of the Experienced Labour Force in the Toronto
Metropolitan Municipality (TMM), Northwestern Ontario (NWO),
and Ontario (ONT)[1].

Occupation	TMM	NWO	ONT
Managerial, Administrative, and			
Related Occupations	12.6	7.9(7.4)[2]	11.2
Teaching and Related Occupations	3.6	4.3(4.2)	4.0
Medicine and Health	4.0	4.6(3.6)	4.4
Technological, Social, Religious and			
Artistic, and Related Occupations	9.8	6.1(5.7)	7.7
Clerical and Related Occupations	22.8	15.6(13.9)	19.1
Sales	9.4	7.8(6.5)	9.1
Service	11.1	15.1(15.9)	11.9
Primary	0.7	6.2(9.6)	3.6
Processing	2.3	5.9(6.3)	3.1
Machining, Product Fabricating,			
Assembling, and Repairing	10.9	8.0(7.3)	11.7
Constructions Trades	4.5	7.9(8.7)	5.5
Transport Equipment Operating	2.6	5.6(6.2)	3.4
Other	5.7	5.1(4.8)	5.3

Source: Calculated from figures in Statistics Canada, 1988.

[1] Due to rounding columns may not total 100 per cent.

[2] The figures in brackets represent northwestern Ontario excluding the city of Thunder Bay.

their physical strength, courage, perseverance, and their drinking binges and spending sprees. Although this may be an invented tradition, some of the values are still dimly present in the male working-class culture of the region. It provides cultural dispositions which are embodied and expressed by young men. The celebration of physical strength, practical skill, the willingness to withstand discomfort stoically, and being able to "drink like a man" become important signifiers of regional identity and distinctiveness.

For many working-class individuals the pulp and paper mills, sawmills, grain elevators, and railroad companies represent the best employment possibilities. Wages are considered to be good, the jobs are unionized, and, until recently, employment seemed secure.[10] When I finished high school in 1973 "everyone" was going to work at The Great Lakes Forest Products mill. Post-secondary education was not required to qualify for a job, although a contact in the mill was often a necessity. The "money was good," especially if you were young with few or no responsibilities to other people.

The distinctiveness of northwestern Ontario vis-à-vis the rest of the province is also illustrated by the ethnic composition of its pop-

Table 3
Population in the Districts of Northwestern Ontario, 1971–86

Year	1986	1981	1976	1971
Kenora	52,835	59,421	57,980	53,230
Rainy River	22,870	22,798	24,768	25,750
Thunder Bay	155,675	153,997	150,647	145,390
Total	231,380	236,216	233,395	224,370

Sources: Statistics Canada 1988; 1982, Table 4; 1973, Table 2.

ulation. In this respect, the region resembles western rather than eastern Canada. After people of British origin (43 per cent), the largest ethnic groups are French Canadian (9 per cent), North American Native (8 per cent), Ukrainian (8 per cent), Italian (6 per cent), and Finnish (5 per cent) (LSPC 1980, 21). The non-British European ethnic groups came to the region to fill the hard, dangerous, insecure, and, at the time, poorly paid jobs in forestry, mining, and construction at the end of the nineteenth century and early in the twentieth (see chapter 5).

HINTERLANDS WITHIN
THE HINTERLAND

More than half the population of northwestern Ontario lives in or around the city of Thunder Bay, located on the northwest shore of Lake Superior at the mouth of the Kaministikwia River. The city, where the bulk of the ethnographic research was carried out, was formed in 1970 when the cities of Port Arthur and Fort William were amalgamated with the townships of McIntyre and Neebing. Thunder Bay's population numbers 112,272, and almost 10,000 more people live in the adjacent townships and on the Fort William Indian reserve which borders the city on the south (TBEDC 1988, c-1).

Northwestern Ontario experienced a population decline in the period 1981–86 after a decade of growth. The economic boom experienced in southern Ontario during the 1980s has not been shared by northwestern Ontario. Between 1981 and 1986 the population of the city of Thunder Bay declined slightly (0.2 per cent), while the surrounding townships grew very slightly (0.2 per cent). During this same period, the population of Canada increased by 4.2 per cent, Ontario by 5.7 per cent, and Toronto by 9.5 per cent. Indeed, all

Table 4
Population in Northwestern Ontario Urban Centres, 1976–86

Year	1986	1981	1976
Atikokan	4,345	4,452	5,803
Fort Frances	8,870	8,906	9,325
Dryden	6,465	6,640	6,799
Kenora	9,620	9,817	10,565
Thunder Bay	112,270	112,486	111,476

Source: Statistics Canada 1988; 1982, Table 4.

the larger cities in northern Ontario, both west and east, declined in population between 1981 and 1986: Sudbury by 4.6 per cent, North Bay 0.7 per cent, and Sault Ste Marie 2.7 per cent (TBEDC 1988, C-2).

The city of Thunder Bay has the most varied economic base in northwestern Ontario. Although there are some exceptions, such as in the vicinity of the Hemlo gold fields, smaller communities in the region are generally experiencing a worsening economic situation. They have also experienced a population decline over the last decade or more.

Smaller towns rely heavily on a single industry such as a mine or a paper mill. Atikokan was devastated by the closure of the Steep Rock iron mine. Fort Frances, Kenora, and Dryden are all heavily dependent on the forest industry, as is Thunder Bay although to a lesser extent. The boom-and-bust cycle typical of industries such as mining and forest products leaves deep traces in communities in northwestern Ontario. Thus, although Thunder Bay's economy was stagnant throughout the 1980s, it was relatively well off compared to many of the small communities in the region.

The most deeply affected are Native communities where unemployment may run as high as ninety per cent, and the social pathologies associated with deplorable economic conditions are taking a heavy toll (Driben and Trudeau 1983; Shkilnyk 1985). While the overall population of the region has declined, the Native population has increased rapidly and is of growing importance throughout northwestern Ontario and in the city of Thunder Bay. Natives form less than one per cent of the population of Ontario, but make up about eight per cent of the population of northwestern Ontario. Given that the Native birth rate in Canada in 1981 was twice the national average, that the Native population is very young (thirty-nine per cent under the age of fifteen), and that there is a shortage of employment and housing, it is not surprising that large numbers of Native people are moving off the reserve. In 1981, thirty per cent of the registered Indian population lived off-reserve (Siggner 1986).

The dire situation in some of the reserve communities in north-western Ontario has been much discussed, in part at least because of the graphic descriptions in Shkilnyk's book (1985) about Grassy Narrows. But the divisions between Native and non-Native communities are striking, even when communities in far better shape than Grassy Narrows are used as the comparative example. Whereas in 1985 median male income in the city of Thunder Bay was $24,396, higher than both the national and provincial median male incomes, across the river on the Fort William Indian reserve it was only $12,624. The comparative figures for women were $9,059 in Thunder Bay and $6,617 on the Fort William reserve. The unemployment rate for both sexes between the ages of fifteen and twenty-four years was 15.1 per cent in the city of Thunder Bay, and 56.3 per cent on the adjacent reserve. For those twenty-four years and over the unemployment figures were 10.3 per cent in Thunder Bay and 28.6 per cent on the reserve (Statistics Canada 1988).[11] Similar contrasts can be drawn across the region. On the one hand, then, there are predominantly white communities where, if the economic base is on an upswing, the inhabitants have incomes which compare favourably to national and provincial norms, and on the other hand, there are native communities where people have significantly lower incomes, and unemployment is a fact of life for a large minority, if not the majority, of the population.

A survey carried out by the Canadian Native Indian Committee on Alcoholism in 1981 found that in the city of Thunder Bay and surrounding area there were 1,301 status Indians (including the Fort William Band), 2,700 non-status Indians and 9,200 Métis. This totals 13,201 or approximately ten per cent of the population of the census metropolitan area of Thunder Bay (LSPC 1983, 4,7). There are few data available on the socio-economic conditions of Natives living in Thunder Bay. However, a report prepared by the Native People of Thunder Bay Development Corporation in June 1983 on the employment and related needs of Native women in Thunder Bay gives some insight into the situation of Native women in the city: 61.5 per cent of the women surveyed for the report were single mothers with an average of 2.68 children; 76.9 per cent were unemployed; the source of income for 63.1 per cent of these women was social assistance; 66.9 per cent had a monthly income of less than $1,000

Table 5
Female Average Employment Income as a Percentage of Male Average
Employment Income for Canada, Ontario, Thunder Bay District (TBD),
Kenora District (KD), and Rainy River District (RRD), 1985.

Type of Employment	Can	Ont	TBD	KD	RRD
Full year/full time	65.5	64.1	59.7	59.0	58.5
Part year/part time	59.5	60.1	45.2	45.3	50.1

Source: Calculated from figures in Statistics Canada 1988.

a month; and the mean annual income was $8,902.68, nearly $9,000 below the National Council of Welfare's poverty line for a family of four.

The differences between the large city and the smaller towns, and between the Native and white communities indicate significant disparities within the region. Running through all these communities, of course, is a strong difference in the economic opportunities available to men and women. The fact that women are worse off than men in terms of income and employment, and that there are female job ghettos, is hardly surprising given the situation of women throughout the country and, indeed, the contemporary Western world.[12]

In northwestern Ontario the imbalance between men and women in terms of income is somewhat more extreme than the national and provincial averages. Female median income in northwestern Ontario is only thirty-eight per cent of male median income, whereas for the country as a whole it is forty-eight per cent, and in Ontario it is forty-seven per cent of male income.[13] Table 5 shows 1985 average employment income for women as a percentage of men's employment income for Canada, Ontario, and the three districts of northwestern Ontario for full-time and part-time work. It illustrates the fact that women's earnings from employment relative to men's are even lower in northwestern Ontario than in the nation or province as a whole, especially for seasonal and part-time female workers. Even within the city of Thunder Bay women's employment income is only sixty per cent of men's.[14]

Women are much more likely to work part of the year or part time than men throughout Canada. The lack of full-time and full-year employment for women is also more marked in northwestern Ontario where two-thirds of all female workers are employed part of the year or part time. Men in northwestern Ontario are also less

Table 6
Occupational Profile (in Percentages) of the Experienced Female Labour Force and Experienced Male Labour Force in Northwestern Ontario.[1]

Occupation	Male	Female
Managerial, Administrative, and Related Occupations	9.0	6.3
Teaching and Related Occupations	2.9	6.4
Medicine and Health	1.1	9.7
Technological, Social, Religious, Artistic, and Related Occupations	6.3	5.7
Clerical and Related Occupations	4.9	30.1
Sales	6.0	10.4
Service	9.6	23.0
Primary	9.3	1.8
Processing	8.9	1.3
Machining, Product Fabricating, Assembling, and Repairing	12.7	1.3
Constructions Trades	13.1	0.5
Transport Equipment Operating	8.5	1.4
Other	7.6	1.4

Source: Calculated from figures in Statistics Canada (1988).

[1] Due to rounding columns may not total 100 per cent.

likely to have full-time year-round employment than men in Ontario and Canada as a whole.[15]

The occupational profile in Table 6 shows that almost two-thirds of women workers in northwestern Ontario are employed in clerical, sales, and service occupations. With the addition of teaching and jobs related to medicine and health, three-quarters of all female workers are accounted for. Women are over-represented in these occupational categories throughout the province and nation. There are some interesting regional variations, however. Clerical and related work forms the largest occupational category for women throughout the province, but it is somewhat less important in northwestern Ontario than in the province as a whole and metropolitan Toronto in particular. On the other hand, service occupations are much more important for women in northwestern Ontario than for women in metropolitan Toronto and the province of Ontario as a whole (see Table 7).

The working class makes its decisions and forms its own sense of meaning, of importance, in this regional context. A woman facing a future serving doughnuts at a coffee shop, or making beds in a hotel, or working on the cash register at K-Mart, may very well

Table 7
Occupational Profile (in Percentages) of the Experienced Female Labour Force in Northwestern Ontario, Ontario, and the Toronto Metropolitan Municipality.[1]

Occupation	TMM	NWO	ONT
Managerial, Administrative and			
Related Occupations	10.3	6.3	8.4
Teaching and Related Occupations	5.0	6.4	5.7
Medicine and Health	6.6	9.7	8.1
Technological, Social, Religious,			
Artistic, and Related Occupations	7.3	5.7	5.9
Clerical and Related Occupations	37.2	30.1	34.0
Sales	8.9	10.4	9.6
Service	11.3	23.0	14.6
Primary	0.3	1.8	1.9
Processing	1.4	1.3	1.7
Machining, Product Fabricating,			
Assembling, and Repairing	7.1	1.3	5.9
Constructions Trades	0.3	0.5	0.3
Transport Equipment Operating	0.4	1.4	0.8
Other	3.9	1.4	3.1

Source: Calculated from figures in Statistics Canada (1988).

[1] Due to rounding columns may not total 100 percent.

earnestly look forward to the day she is married to a man with a steady job at the mill, or perhaps a skilled trade. For young men growing up in this environment, the culturally appropriate and most realistic course is often to grab onto an available job and begin to acquire some seniority and whatever security and benefits come with it.

The differences between northwestern Ontario and the rest of the province, especially metropolitan Toronto, the symbolic image of "the South," are in many respects a matter of degree rather than kind. But they are real, and provide a structure within which people live, and through which they construct their own sense of identity. Women and men live in and through their culture, and that culture is continually formed and re-formed in the seemingly minor details of everyday life. In northwestern Ontario the details of that everyday life contain the dominant, residual, and emergent traces of the region's hinterland status.

PART THREE

Resistance, Reaction, and Hegemonic Closure

CHAPTER FOUR

The Tournament

INTRODUCTION

The importance of the ordinary, the prosaic as opposed to the poetic, is especially evident in the leisure activities of the Boys. They have no interest in high culture, but they are captivated by the so-called low culture of the masses. Anything that is esoteric is élitist from their point of view. Thus, mass culture is perceived as democratic because it does not exclude anyone, rather than as an example of the degradation of culture in the modern world.

Leisure time is relatively free and because of this the activities pursued during leisure time are useful places to begin a description and analysis of the cultural themes important to the working class. In modern wage labour social and cultural desires are at best considered irrelevant and at worst actively suppressed by the rationale of the labour process. The social and cultural needs and wants of workers are generally seen as antithetical to the efficient execution of the labour process; if they are valued at all it is only to the extent they may be harnessed to the increase of productivity.[1] For this reason central working-class concerns, many of which are developed through work, are displaced to the ritual and symbolic activity of leisure (Clarke 1976, 176). Therefore, if one intends to analyze expressions of working-class culture, what working-class individuals do during their free time outside of their wage labour is a logical focus. Symbols and rituals of the leisure sphere can be interpreted as rituals which reveal the values held dear by the working class, just as Balinese cockfights express what it means to be Balinese (Geertz 1975a).

The freedom of leisure time is by no means absolute, but in the context of an industrial capitalist social formation it is relatively free of the constraints which characterize wage labour for the working class.[2] "Free time" is governed by informal and formal codes, ranging from unspoken ideas about what constitutes correct behaviour in any given context to the laws which control when, where, how, and with whom leisure time can be spent. While the idea that leisure time is free must be understood in this limited sense, it is, nonetheless, the time when the working class is not under the direct control of the labour process and is better able to express itself and pursue its own desires (Clarke 1976, 175).

This is not to suggest that wage labour is not a central feature of working-class life; indeed, it is one of the defining features of the working class. Nor is it to suggest that working-class culture is not also constituted in and through the experience of wage labour. As I argue later in the text, the experience of work is constitutive of working-class ideas about knowledge, and these in turn provide the substratum upon which notions of how leisure time should be spent and the kinds of cultural activities that are enjoyable are constructed.

Moreover, however alienating the experience of wage labour is, it is well established that workers do actively attempt to fill the experience of work with meaning. They turn the labour process into a game (Burawoy 1979b, 77–94), they contest management's imposition of scientific management techniques, and they construct their own definitions of worth in part around their work. All of these practices are cultural as well as political, and the values constituted through them are carried from the shopfloor into the wider world. Thus, it would be absurd to try to understand the leisure sphere in isolation from the world of work. In the discussion that follows, the inescapable fact of wage labour must be kept in mind as the context in which leisure takes place.

Sports are among the most popular leisure activities today in many parts of the world and certainly in North America and Western Europe. Few events attract as many spectators as professional or high-level amateur sports, and few individuals gain the renown of top-calibre athletes. There is often a deep emotional and intellectual commitment on the part of fans and participants. The fortunes of teams and players are followed religiously. People have been moved to riot and nations to war over the outcome of games or the treatment of players.[3]

The Boys are very interested in sport, both as spectators and participants. Watching and playing sports are major leisure activities, although by no means are they the Boys' only leisure interests. From mid-May until the end of August lob-ball, a form of softball, was the main focus of the Boys' attention during time off work. They played at least twice a week and often on weekends, and sometimes would go to watch games on other evenings. Unlike spectator sports and other public rituals which are in the control of the dominant social groups in society, lob-ball is the Boys' game. It is a dramatic spectacle, however mundane it may appear to outsiders, in which they act out the values of their own culture.[4]

THE LEISURE OF THE BOYS

As a means of contextualizing the discussion of softball, I want to begin with a general description of the leisure practices of the Boys. As I have said, it is important to keep in mind that leisure is circumscribed by work. Forty or more hours of each week must be spent in wage labour with the exception of holidays or periods of unemployment. The necessity of wage labour is always present, and for the Boys it involves fixed hours. Unlike academics, say, who are to some extent able to adjust their own work schedules to accommodate their chosen domestic routine and leisure activities, the Boys must follow the schedule established by management. They do try to arrange holidays to fit their own wishes, but young workers are generally low on the seniority list and frequently must take holiday periods which their older colleagues do not want. Those who work shifts trade with fellow workers, but this usually demands management's approval and opportunities to trade are limited since many workers prefer to have weekends and evenings off. One can rarely gain more favourable hours of leisure by trading shifts; one merely exchanges one weekend or evening for another. The skilled tradesmen among the Boys were frequently employed out of the city and thus could not return at will to participate in leisure activities with their friends. Tradesmen working in construction could choose their own holiday times, and would do so when work was abundant. But this freedom was curtailed when jobs were scarce and they had to take what employment was available, even if it meant rearranging or cancelling holiday plans.

The Boys have a variety of leisure pursuits. In terms of the number of hours spent on a given activity, watching television may be the most important. As in many modern homes, the Boys' living-rooms are arranged around the television, symbolizing its importance in the household.

But television does not absorb as much leisure time as this may suggest. The television is on virtually all the time when people are in the dwelling, but it is not necessarily being watched attentively. Television provides a background or complement to other activities.

For example, the television is turned on as soon as the householders return from work, but the woman of the house frequently prepares dinner, while the man may sit and read the paper. The television is left on during dinner but again as a backdrop rather than a focus of attention.

After dinner, if the couple are not going out they may sit and watch television. Normally, though, while there are certain shows which are preferred and attentively watched, television falls by and large into the background while the couple engage in other activities. For the women, these might include doing the laundry, ironing clothes, knitting, or preparing lunches for the next day; for those with children, there are the many tasks involved in child care. The men, although less involved in the day-to-day domestic labour, do a lot of "puttering." For people with homes, there is grass to cut or snow to shovel and a variety of minor home repairs. If friends come over to visit the television is usually left on unless they decide to listen to the stereo. Conversation or a game of cards or backgammon takes place against the background of the television. Television is thus an important component of leisure but is actually watched with attention only part of the time it is on.

Another important leisure activity, at least in terms of the time it takes, is shopping. Not all shopping can be thought of as leisure. Going for groceries is a regular weekly domestic duty, and shopping for clothes for the family and other household needs is part of the domestic economy. As such shopping tends to be viewed as women's work. In Thunder Bay this involves going to a large supermarket often located in a shopping mall. There are few small local shops, consequently grocery shopping is very inconvenient without a car.

Shopping purely as a leisure activity is more common for women than for men. Women often go shopping while boyfriends or husbands watch sports on television or go to a bar with their friends. But shopping is not exclusively a woman's activity, nor does it necessarily entail actual buying. Rather, it involves going to the mall and wandering through the stores, perhaps stopping for a coffee, especially if, as frequently happens, one meets friends. For some commentators the destruction of small community shops, the creation of suburbia, and the rise of shopping malls are indicative of the decline of working-class communities and a distinctive working-class culture. But in Thunder Bay, where the winter is long and cold, the mall is a place for socializing. Jerry Jacobs (1984) views shopping malls as places where one attempts to escape reality. But, together with automobiles, without which malls could not exist, they also provide a means for overcoming, to a small extent, the individuation of modern life.

Social drinking is an important part of life for the local working class, especially for young workers who do not have children and therefore have more free time and money. Drinking follows a regular pattern which is related to the weekly and yearly cycle of social activities. If there is heavy drinking, it normally takes place on the weekends, while during the week people generally abstain, or perhaps restrict their drinking to an occasional beer after work. This short-term cyclical pattern intersects with a longer cycle revolving around yearly rituals, including the society-wide annual celebrations such as Christmas, and the specific annual activities peculiar to different informal groups – the "tourney weekends" for the Boys (see below), or perhaps the annual hunting or fishing trip for many others. At these times, people may drink quite heavily several days in a row.

Alcohol, among the Boys at least, was not appreciated in and of itself. They are not lone drinkers. One is always offered a beer or sometimes a drink of hard liquor when visiting, but it is rare for the Boys to sit by themselves and have a drink. They are not "connoisseurs" of wine, beer, or liquor. One either drinks to get drunk, or at least to relax, or one does not drink at all. In this sense, drinking among the young male working class approximates the pattern of binge drinking.

It is common for people to "go out drinking" at least once a week. One young couple, for example, budgeted forty dollars a week for Friday night in the bar. Generally, men drink more than women on any given night out, and go out drinking more often than women. Indeed, the women, when they accompanied their husbands or boyfriends to the bar, often had to "take it easy" so they could drive home, and because female drunkenness, while not unusual, still carries a stigma it does not for males. Going out drinking is a group activity. Individuals or couples, even if they initially go alone, expect to meet friends at the bar. As described below, drinking is also an aspect of other leisure activities such as participatory sports.

There are a variety of bars in Thunder Bay, ranging from those which charge a cover fee and have a dress code to the working-class bars where people can dress casually and just sit and drink beer. The informality of the latter is favoured by the Boys, although they also patronize other types of bars from time to time. They distinguish between more and less respectable bars, and prefer those where they feel the atmosphere is relaxed and unpretentious, yet where symbols of poverty do not exist.[5]

Hunting and fishing are also popular leisure activities in Thunder Bay. The degree of interest varies, of course, from individual to individual. Some couples spend as much time as possible camping and fishing. Both the men and women enjoy the outdoors and they often spend a considerable amount of money on four-wheel-drive vehicles, boats, motors, campers for the back of trucks, and fishing equipment. The typical pattern for the Boys, however, was to make a couple of weekend-long fishing trips during the summer. Sometimes this was a male-only event, but wives and girlfriends often went along.

Participatory sports of various kinds are very popular in northwestern Ontario. A study of communities of 1,000 or more people in the region conducted in 1982 by the Ontario Ministry of Tourism and Recreation (MTR) found that forty-four per cent of the sample population participated in forty-five different sports. This excludes sports which do not have a minimal form of organization, such as road hockey or sand-lot baseball.

The study differentiated between casual sport, which was structured by the players themselves on an *ad hoc* basis (e.g., pay-as-you-play hockey or randomly-booked squash games); organized sport, which has some form of administrative structure and regular competition (e.g., house leagues); competitive sport, which involves regular and organized skill instruction, practice time, and advanced competition; and élite sport, which is aimed at maximizing the performance levels of the participants through high-quality instruction, regular practice, and competition at provincial, national or international levels.

The most popular categories by far are casual and organized sport, which involve some 67,318 participants, or eighty per cent of the MTR study's sample. The age category of twenty-three to thirty-five years had the highest number of participants in sport, and there was a two-to-one ratio of male to female participants in all categories. The eight most common organized sports in northwestern Ontario were, in order of frequency, five-pin bowling, ice hockey, golf, softball, curling, baseball, soccer, and shooting. In five-pin bowling women outnumber men, but in the other seven sports men outnumber women. Ice hockey and shooting are almost exclusively male activities (Ontario n.d.).

SOFTBALL AND ITS VARIATIONS

The kind of softball played by the Boys falls into the category of organized sport; there is a league structure but it is not competitive in the sense of demanding regular training and practice with an eye to improving so as consistently to beat the opponent. In the summers of 1984, 1985, and 1986 the city was alive with softball fever.[6] Every evening from Monday through Thursday from the beginning of June to the middle of August, the numerous baseball fields in Thunder Bay were occupied. On most weekends there was at least one tournament. An employee of the MTR in the city estimated that there were in excess of three hundred teams (personal communication).

Various kinds of baseball and softball are played in the city. There is a senior hardball league, but it consists of only three teams and draws very few spectators, if any. There are also little-league teams for children between the ages of six and sixteen which also feature hardball modelled on the style of the professional major leagues. It is played with a small hardball which is pitched overhand. There is also a fastball league. In this version of the game the ball is pitched underhand at a high velocity, and good pitchers have a repertoire of pitches – curves, sinkers, change-ups, and fastballs, to name a few.

But the largest number of people are interested in a kind of softball that requires less skill and is therefore open to a larger segment of the population. There are two varieties: slo-pitch and lob-ball. In the former, a larger ball than that used in fastball is pitched under-hand toward the plate. Balls and strikes are called by an umpire as in regular hardball, but there is a rule governing the speed of the pitch. In practice this a frequent subject of dispute between the teams and the umpire. The goal, however, is to make it relatively easy to hit the ball. A larger ball, approximately thirty-five centimetres in diameter, is employed in lob-ball. As the name implies, the ball is lobbed in a high arc rather than thrown across a plate. Balls and strikes are determined by whether or not the ball lands on a mat placed against the plate, rather than by the path of the ball over the plate.

Other rule changes also make the game easier to play. There are ten players on the field rather than nine as in standard baseball. The extra player is normally used as a fourth fielder, although there is no specific rule governing his or her positioning. To speed up the game, two strikes make an out, and three balls make a walk. A foul ball on the last strike is an out. There is a "mercy rule." If after five innings one team is leading by fifteen or more runs, a not unusual circumstance in my experience, the game is over. In the "mixed leagues" each team must have at least three women on the field at all times.

The rule changes have the overall effect of making the game easier and faster to play, but this does not mean the games are not competitive. The players hope to win, and decisions made by the umpires are sometimes the subject of heated argument. Indeed, within the various slo-pitch and lob-ball leagues there is a gradation in the level of competitiveness and the seriousness with which the players approach the game. Every team has its "star" and its less illustrious players. Individual teams sometimes have problems because some players are concerned with winning, while others are there simply to have fun.

Generally, though, fun is the point of the whole exercise. Anyone who takes the competitive element of these games too seriously is frowned upon. There is an unwritten, but nonetheless understood, set of rules governing appropriate behaviour. Efforts are made to avoid body contact in, for example, close plays at home plate or first base; one does not express disappointment too strongly over an error or when striking out; and one does not publicly criticize other people's play. These rules are frequently transgressed. The only means of enforcing them is through ostracism, gossip, and name-calling. Post-game discussions are often centred on such matters – "So-and-so was a real asshole tonight," or, "X is a goddamn jerk." The fine line between not trying hard enough and thereby ruining the competitiveness of the game, and playing more intensely than is considered appropriate and thereby lessening the fun, must be continually negotiated by the participants. Individuals who are more serious about athletics, skill levels, and competition play hardball, fastball, or other more demanding sports. Serious athletes who play in the slo-pitch or lob-ball leagues must carefully judge their behaviour if they wish to avoid derision, for these games are not intended to be taken too seriously, at least not if it ruins the fun for others. Such players are particularly apt to be seen as prima donnas since, it is thought, the only reason they play at this level is to show off.

The working-class bar that sponsors the league in which the Boys play is very popular. It is reputed to be the busiest drinking establishment between Sudbury and Winnipeg. A local representative of one of the major breweries informed me that it is certainly the busiest bar in the city in terms of the quantity of beer sold.

Sponsorship of the league means the bar provides funds for field equipment such as the bases and home plate, and helps cover the cost of the league tournament by supplying trophies, beer, and food. The financial commitment is not large, in the hundreds rather than thousands of dollars. In a spirit of generalized reciprocity (Sahlins 1972, 193–4) many teams' members regularly drink beer at the bar after games. Normally, one team member is responsible for bringing a case of beer to the diamond. When the game is completed, the team members, along with girlfriends, wives, and friends, gather around the back of someone's pickup truck, drink beer, and discuss the game, or just "shoot the shit." When the beer is gone or it begins to get dark someone suggests going to the bar and, in my experience, at least a few individuals always take up the suggestion. The bar is conveniently located in relation to the league diamond, and if five

or more team members in uniform are present the bar provides one
or two free pizzas, depending on the number of people.

Teams must find their own sponsors. In the league that the Boys
play in there are eight teams and all but two have sponsors.[7] These
include an electrical-parts equipment dealership, a gas station, a
bowling alley, an automobile garage, a pizza restaurant, and a road-
house-style bar/restaurant. The amount of money donated by the
sponsors varies and each team spends it as it wishes. The Boys'
sponsor gave them two hundred dollars with which they purchased
bats and balls and paid part of the team's entry fee for a tournament.
Other teams bought uniforms, or at least covered part of the cost.
The sponsor receives publicity from having the company name in
the newspaper one night a week when league standings are published, or perhaps from being mentioned on the late-night sports
news on television. Some teams also had the sponsor's name on their
uniforms.

Even with corporate sponsorship, participation in the lob-ball league can involve significant personal expense. The Boys bought their
own uniforms at a cost of between $70 and $80 each.[8] Baseball
gloves range in price from $40 to $100 or more. Shoes, in some
cases baseball cleats, cost on average $30 to $60 a pair. There is an
individual league entry fee of $10. In addition, there are the regular
contributions to the team's beer fund, money spent at the bar, tournament entry fees, hotel costs for those who go away for a tournament, and money spent on beer and food at tournaments, not to
mention incidental expenses such as the gasoline used driving to
and from the baseball diamond. It is impossible to make a strict
calculation of the cost involved in playing lob-ball because individual
habits vary, but for the basic equipment an expenditure of between
$100 and $200 is required. A minimum of $20 a week is spent on
beer, and more than this when there is a weekend tournament. Given
that with playoffs the season lasts three to four months, the cost of
a summer of softball is easily $400 to $500, and may be considerably
higher depending on how actively one participates in the social activities associated with the games. Of course, uniforms, gloves, and
shoes are not purchased every year so the cost decreases after the
first year, and in some cases sponsors' contributions defray the expense of uniforms. Many of the Boys also participate in winter sports
such as hockey which also involve outlays for equipment and the
social "extras." A year of sport, even at this recreational level can
easily cost $1,000 and more.

The teams are based on informal groups. There are no team
tryouts as in competitive sports. Although each team is allowed a
roster of only twenty players, no one is ever prevented from playing

on the basis of his ability. The teams are composed of friends and that is the only criterion for belonging. Friendships cross team boundaries as well, linking all the teams in the league. In the bar after games the players of each team along with girlfriends, wives, and friends arrange the tables so that everyone can sit together. A "table" may consist of anywhere between two and thirty people. As the evening progresses people move about, visiting friends at other tables. On "good" nights the boundaries between tables dissolve and the entire bar is transformed into one extended informal group.

THE GAME[9]

On a hot Tuesday night in July several of the Boys were gathered around the "dugout." The dugout consisted of a simple wooden bench. In the preceding years the baseball diamond had been repeatedly vandalized. Wooden dugouts were destroyed so the athletic association that manages the diamond had new ones constructed of cement blocks, but these were also demolished. The Boys were convinced that Indians from the nearby reservation were responsible, although no one was actually caught in the act.

Three girlfriends sat quietly behind the Boys in the bleachers. Besides being committed fans, the girlfriends and wives sometimes acted as scorekeepers and were often, as previously noted, designated drivers if their mates drank too much after the game. Across the field, the other team's dugout and bleachers looked exactly the same.

In addition to the girlfriends or wives, the only other spectators were two young Ojibwa boys who were climbing in and out of a wooden structure built behind the backstop. With the arrival of the teams that were to play in the second game the scene became more lively.

From the bench which served as a dugout one of the Boys offered me a beer. It was not unusual for the players to "warm up" with a beer or a cigarette, and even to sip a beer and have a smoke between innings or while waiting for their turn at bat.

The diamond was a ramshackle affair. The infield was gravel, making slides a courageous act. The outfield was natural grass in the full sense of the term, complete with clover and crab grass like the nearby fields. The infield was raked sporadically to maintain a semblance of evenness, and the outfield was mowed occasionally. The rough terrain caused the ball to take bizarre bounces from time to time. Footing could be treacherous in the outfield. After a rainstorm large puddles formed and players had to stand ankle-deep in the water to play their position correctly. Wooden boards served as the outfield fence. They were in dire need of paint and some, torn down by vandals, had to be replaced. In right field, where the distance to the fence was shortest, an eight-foot wall had been constructed of pressboard to make it more difficult to hit home runs. "The Dogs," which was the nickname of the previous year's league champion, was scrawled across the wall with orange spray paint. The name referred to the Husky dog on the logo of the service station that sponsored the team.

The game was late in starting. The umpires, who were members of a team playing in the next game, had not yet arrived. The Boys were restless. They had already warmed up.

Despite individual differences in shape and size, the Boys and other players in the league exemplified a body type which was emphatically not the lean, fit look of the health-and-fitness subculture, but rather closer to the "beefcake" variety. Some had already grown beer bellies despite their relative youth. As I have already indicated, strength and power are valued in their culture and this is expressed in an appreciation of body size. As important as strength and power, however, is the obvious lack of concern for fitness. This is meat-and-potatoes-and-beer territory. Despite their team uniforms, few players looked athletic. Nobody cared much, certainly not those who sat on the dugout bench drinking a beer and smoking a cigarette, waiting for the game to begin.

Another team member ambled in from the parking lot. His movements were typical of the body technique of the Boys, which reflects the high value placed on the maintenance of expressive control. In the context of the lob-ball game, professional baseball players serve as a model; perhaps more than other professional athletes, they exude a casual air which is echoed in the Boys' style of movement. A great deal of effort is put into appearing casual. One does not want to give the impression of being too eager or of trying too hard. This attitude and the accompanying body technique are part of shopfloor culture, but they are also related to the fact that popularity is partly based on being good at a wide range of practical skills and physical activities without seeming to work at them. As I already stated, anyone seriously involved in competitive athletics participates in other sports.

However, the Boys' style also reflects the macho male culture of the region. Northwestern Ontario is a place of long, empty distances, of big machinery, large trucks, rail cars, and lake ships. These objects provide models and metaphors for the human body. Size and power are important aspects of the ideal body type. To be built "like a brick shithouse" is a positive attribute in the Boys' world, but it is not because they worship body building.

Indeed, the ideal man in this world is someone who is physically strong and well coordinated, and skillful at practical tasks; who is "not afraid of work" and doesn't "take any shit"; who does not complain about physical inconvenience – in other words, someone who is tough, physically and emotionally. As I mentioned earlier, there is an echo of the ethos of workmen in the staple economy in contemporary working-class culture. The first working-class people in the region were miners, loggers, and labourers on large construction projects such as the building of the railroads. The work was physically demanding and the living conditions in the camps were often primitive. In these conditions one had to be physically and emotionally tough, and relatively self-reliant. Work and living conditions have improved greatly, but as metaphors of masculinity these values remain important, especially for men in early adulthood who have not yet acquired the other signs of masculinity – the wife, children, and home.

As he entered the dugout, Sam,[10] the new arrival, was greeted with: "What the fuck are you doing here? I thought you went to Dryden?" Sam responded as he lit a cigarette, "I did. They promised me at the [union] hall we would have private rooms. But when I got there they wanted to make the single guys share, so I said 'fuck it.' Anyway, we got a big game tonight." He smiled. Sam is a tradesman. He had been unemployed for several months, but, as he put it, he "didn't need the kind of bullshit [his] employer wanted to pull." Sam is big and strong, and athletically gifted.

The game began and, like all the lob-ball games I watched and played in, it was a mixture of skillful, humorous, and pathetic plays. One moment there was a diving catch of a line drive, only to be followed by an easy fly ball that popped out of the fielder's glove. The effects of a well-executed doubleplay were negated when the shortstop picked up a routine ground ball and threw it twenty feet over the head of the first baseman. A running catch on a long fly ball came to nought when the fielder dropped the ball over the fence, thereby giving up a home run. The highlight of this game, for me, came when Sam made a long, running catch on a fly ball without removing the cigarette from his lips.

Although few players or teams ever made serious efforts to improve their play through practice or training, or by avoiding the bar the night before – to do so might verge on being too eager – games were taken seriously in the sense that tempers flared and a real hostility sometimes developed between opposing team players, and between the players and the umpires.

On this particular evening the Boys won handily. As the next game's teams took over the bench that served as a dugout, we moved to the parking lot where one of the team members had a case of beer in the back of his half-ton. As we hung around the back of the truck drinking beer, the conversation turned to who was going to the bar that sponsors the league. It was rare to have fewer than six of the Boys stop in the bar and take advantage of the free pizzas. The bar was a favourite with all kinds of teams, whether they played in the league or not, as well as with the crowd from the Wednesday-night stock-car races, and the men coming off their shifts at the nearby paper mill, grain elevators, rail yards, and the light-transit car factory. A couple of the Boys said they could not come and were immediately barraged with insults. Work in the morning was no excuse, although it certainly did have a bearing on how "hard" the night would be.[11]

The bar has managed to maintain something of its earlier community atmosphere, despite heavy commercialization and "improvements" such as a giant television screen and a regular disc jockey. During a long bitter strike by the Canadian Paperworkers Union in 1976, the bar provided free coffee and sandwiches to the strikers, and one can still sometimes see three generations of men – grandfathers, fathers, and sons – sitting together at a table. The current owners are on a first-name basis with most of their clientele, as was their father who owned and managed the bar before them.

The interior of the bar was decorated in a baroque-kitsch style. The walls of pressboard imitation-wood panelling were adorned with plastic clocks and neon signs bearing the insignia and names of different brands of beer, stuffed fish, and photographs of the stock-car the bar sponsors. There was a large trophy case which contained stuffed birds, trophies won by teams sponsored by the bar, union insignia, and a Kinsmen (service club) flag on one wall. A colour television sat atop the trophy case. In one corner there was a huge television screen that was usually tuned to a sports or rock-video station. Another neon sign flashed the names (such as "Ballbuster" and "Orgasm") and prices of "shooters," drinks composed of a mixture of liqueurs and hard liquor, and the time when "shooter hour" began. The style of interior decoration in the bar was similar to that in the "rec rooms" of many local houses.

Thursday to Saturday nights a deejay played music from 9:00 PM until 1:00 AM when the bar closed. There was a small dance floor, as well as a shuffle-board table, a table-hockey game, and a couple of video games.

Those patrons not wearing a team uniform or work clothes were dressed in blue jeans and T-shirts for the most part. Many of the men wore baseball caps, some with team and others with corporate insignia. The waitresses wore white T-shirts with the name of the bar across the front, white jeans and running shoes. One of them was the centre of attention as she tossed empty beer cans into a garbage container from several yards away. Whenever she missed there was a cheer from the onlookers.

As we settled around a table in the bar, it was noted that one member of the gang whose girlfriend had been at the game had decided not to come. "He's such a suckhole these days," my neighbour on the left commented, the implication being that he was dominated by his girlfriend.

After several beers, conversation began to flow as the Boys loosened up and became more expressive. It zipped back and forth between all kinds of subjects and was heavily spiced with jokes and humorous insults of the "bathroom" variety. As was frequently the case, the bulk of the conversation was a retelling for the umpteenth time of the escapades of several of the Boys during a recent weekend – how much they drank, how one of them lost his wallet, how one of them passed out in the back seat of a car, and how a woman had tried to pick one of them up. The stories were told over and over again and seemed to become funnier with each telling; at least the Boys laughed harder each time. Of course, to those who were not actually there, the humour would seem less obvious. Such stories are a way of defining the group. Those who belong understand the humour.

As more beer was consumed, the noise level increased. Someone had only a twenty-dollar bill, and so paid for a round. There were ten of us, plus two girlfriends. Not wanting to break the cycle of reciprocity, all of us but one took turns buying a round.

THE TOURNEY WEEKEND[12]

A highlight of the lob-ball season in Thunder Bay for the Boys was the weekend tournament. There were tournaments almost every weekend through June, July, and August. The Boys entered four tournaments, three in the city and one in a nearby American city.

Tournaments were usually sponsored by one of the large beer companies or a local hotel or bar. There were "mixed" tournaments, in which the teams included both men and women, and others where the teams were either all male or all female. Normally, they began on a Friday night and continued through to Sunday afternoon or evening when the winners were determined. Given the shortage of time, there was often a no-postponement rule, so games were played regardless of the weather unless there was lightning.

As with the games, no two tournaments were exactly alike, but the description of the following tournament includes features common to all the "tourney weekends." It also illustrates a number of elements in the Boys' culture, for "tourney weekends" are a local version of carnival, a two-day party.

The Boys looked forward to this "tourney weekend" with a great deal of excitement. A certain amount of planning was required: entrance fees had to be collected from those who wanted to play, women had to be chosen for the team since this was a mixed tournament, and time off work had to be booked or shifts traded by those scheduled to work over the weekend.

The Boys prepared themselves mentally by alternately expounding the need to avoid excessive partying if they were going to win and retelling stories of last year's tourney weekend escapades. The latter sent them all into fits of laughter as they reminded one another of their antics. Apparently, several team members, after drinking into the early hours of the morning, had slept in the outfield so they would not miss a 9:00 AM game. The next morning they were dirty, smelly, and hungover, but proud that they were on time.

Choosing the women for the team was a contentious affair. A debate developed over whether several of the girlfriends should be asked to play, or whether the Boys should approach other women they knew who regularly played on a women's or mixed team. There was also the question of what positions the "girls" would be allowed to play, where they would do "the least damage to the team," as one of the Boys put it. These issues were never resolved; a few girlfriends and other women were asked to join the team for the tournament and the Boys never did agree ahead of time on what positions they would play.

The tournament was held at the diamond used by the league in which the Boys' team regularly played, although some of the tournament games were located at a second diamond on the nearby reservation. Teams from all over the city participated.

The first games of the tournament were played Friday night. By seven o'clock the parking lot at the diamond was full and the outfield fence was ringed with half-ton trucks and cars. People sat on lawn chairs in the back of the trucks or reclined on the trunks of cars drinking beer and soaking up the evening sun. Children raced up and down the trail around the diamond on their bicycles. Bruce Springsteen, The Cars, and zz Top blared from car stereos.

The Boys played in the second game of the evening. They lost the game, in part, at least, because several of them were so convinced of the incompetence of the women that they would not throw the ball to them. Thus, what should have been several easy outs turned into runs scored as the Boys tried to chase down base runners rather than throw the ball to the women.

After the game, the teams moved to the hall which was located next to the ball diamond. Inside, beer, hot dogs, and hamburgers were sold. The hall was a simple, rectangular building of grey cement blocks. It contained kitchen facilities, washrooms, and rows of long tables. The cement blocks were unpainted and there were no windows, so it was a drab and gloomy building.

The team settled around a table and began the post-mortem on the game. When it became evident that there was a certain amount of tension over the way the women on the team had or had not been "used," a couple of the Boys who were angry with everyone else moved to one end of the table with their girlfriends and continued the conversation, while the others went to get more beer.

There were several teams in the hall and as the sun went down more people moved in. Around ten o'clock someone decided that music was needed, so he backed his car into the open delivery doors at one end of the hall and turned the volume on the car stereo to maximum. Soon, even though the music was so loud it was impossible to talk without shouting, conversation became much more amiable and the jokes and sexual innuendoes began to flow.

When I left just before midnight the whole team was there, still proclaiming its intention to take it easy since we had to win the next day if we wanted to get into the playoff round. In the tournaments, teams must provide people to act as umpires for games in which they are not playing. It was my turn in the morning. As I got up to leave, one of them reminded me that I was to umpire a game played on the baseball diamond at the nearby Indian reserve. The reserve is also known as the Mission, since it was the site of a Jesuit mission established in 1849. "Bring your bows and arrows tomorrow, you're going to the Mission," I was reminded as I went out the door.

The next morning was a beautiful sunny day, with a deep blue, crystal-clear sky. I arrived at the diamond, which sits at the foot of Mount McKay, before anyone else. Ojibwa legend says that Thunder Bird lives on top of the mountain.

The towering mountain with its granite cliffs, the bright green of the vegetation in the early summer, and the blue sky stood in abrupt juxtaposition to the dilapidated community centre and the baseball diamond located behind it. The community centre was old and dirty. The windows had all been shattered and the openings covered with pressboard, the bandage for the wounds society inflicts on old buildings. The stairs were crooked and the door, suspended by one hinge, hung at an angle. Grafitti had been spray-painted over the walls.

The diamond was just as sorry a sight. The outfield fence was broken down in several places. The field was uneven and full of potholes. The outfield grass was ankle-high and the infield was a very soft sand-and-gravel mixture. There were no anchors for the bases and the stands, backstop, and fence were unpainted. The weathered plywood of the outfield board bore the spray-painted names of several heavy-metal rock bands, AC/DC, Quiet Riot, and so on. Home plate faced Mount McKay which stood majestically over the whole scene, and as I sat waiting for the teams and other umpires to arrive a hawk circled lazily, floating on the air currents.

The other umpires, two of the Boys, arrived at the same time as the teams. A young Native man and two small children sat in the stands. As Dick got out of his car he put his sunglasses on. "I think I'm bleeding to death through my eyes," he said. "Hard night?" I inquired. "Not bad, I got three hour's sleep." Floyd carried a Macdonald's orange juice over from his truck. "This is how bad it is. I can't believe I had a Macdonald's breakfast." He took a drink of the orange juice, suddenly became very pale, and ran to the nearest bush.

The first game was played quickly. One team gained a huge lead and we invoked the mercy rule after five innings. In between games Dick and Floyd drove to the other diamond to get some beer from the hall. While they were gone, the next two teams arrived and began their warm-up. Members of one of the teams announced their arrival by roaring into the parking area in a half-ton truck, wildly fishtailing, and screeching to a halt inches from the backstop. Three team members crawled out of the back of the truck, apparently unaware of the danger they had been in. Several of the players were obviously still intoxicated from the night before. One of them said to me, "We practise not sleeping on the weekends."

This game was quite close and I had a few tense moments as both teams told me in no uncertain language I did not know what I was doing as umpire. Actually, they were correct since I did not know, in a formal sense, what the rules were. The three of us who were acting as umpires were following what we understood the rules to be from watching and playing games, not from a knowledge of written rules. Although arguments about rules were common, I never saw anyone refer to a rule book. The biggest dispute of the game erupted when a fly ball bounced off the shoulder of a fielder and over the fence, or where the fence would have been if it had been standing. Was it a double or a home run?

Eventually, the effects of a sleepless and intoxicated night caught up with one of the teams. Their defeat was appropriately symbolized when a fly ball was hit to one of the fielders who was still feeling the effects of the night before. Because he was having such trouble moving, the other umpires had nicknamed him Jim Morrison after the late lead singer of the rock group The Doors who was known to be a heavy drug user. He did a couple of drunken pirouettes while looking into the sky for the ball and then collapsed in a heap. The ball landed on the exposed white flesh of his stomach. Two young Ojibwa boys who were leaning on one of the upright outfield fences doubled over with laughter.

By the time the game ended it was noon and we went to the main diamond for a lunch of hot dogs and beer. The reward for my morning's work was two beer tickets. The parking lot was full. As on the previous evening, the ball park had taken on the aura of a beach. The boards surrounding the outfield were ringed with vehicles again. People were sitting or lying in the backs of trucks or on cars drinking beer, watching the game in progress, and sunbathing. A steady banter flowed between the audience and the outfielders, many of whom were good friends. The verbal exchanges were encouragements for good plays, mild insults, and ironic praise – the bigger the error, the more grandiose the applause. Periodically, one of the outfielders came over to the fence for a sip of someone's beer or a drag on a cigarette. As I stood watching the game and enjoying the sun two fielders ran into each other trying to catch a fly ball. Neither made the catch and the audience sent up a huge cheer. The two players started to call each other Daryl, in reference to characters in the "Bob Newhart Show."[13] The onlookers joined in.

A moment later a home run careened over the fence and struck a woman on the head as she sunbathed on the hood of a car. Apparently, she was unhurt. She immediately jumped up, rubbed her head, and, standing on the hood of the car, made a bow to the rest of the crowd who cheered.

I found a spot to lean on the outfield fence. Two fellows who played for another team in the same league as the Boys stood beside me. They were having a discussion about various people's drinking habits and when it was best to drink what. They knew someone who never drank anything but beer, and even though he drank it all day he never got drunk.

As I turned to look around, I noticed two of the Boys who apparently had been standing behind me for some time. One of them, laughing, yelled at me, "We must stink, eh?" He came over, grabbed my buttocks and said, "That's nice." The other one said to me, "I told you he's a fucking fag." "Look who is talking," came the reply,

"I feel sorry for your old lady [i.e., girlfriend]. Maybe I should go and visit her." "Go ahead. You wouldn't know what to do anyway." "Nah, after she had me she wouldn't want to go back to that puny thing of yours, then you'd be pissed off." "Listen to the bullshit!" he said and, turning his back to the other, he farted and pretended to throw his beer on the other one.

A van pulled up behind us. A little Native boy got out and stood on tiptoes trying to see over the fence. He called to his Grampa who was driving the van. Grampa was a tall thin man, dressed in pointed cowboy boots, pressed blue jeans, a plaid cowboy shirt, a shoelace tie, and a tall, straw Stetson with a feather in one side. Grampa asked his grandson if he could see his Mom, and then tried to point her out to him. Mom was playing for the team on the field. They wore black and yellow uniforms like the Pittsburgh Pirates, with crests on them that said "Olde Union Pub." When Grampa and his grandson wandered off to find a seat in the bleachers behind the team benches, one of the Boys beside me took off his baseball cap and rubbed his hair. "Just checking to see if its all still there," he said, and then he put me in a headlock and said, "Kiss me."

The Boys had a game that afternoon at three o'clock on the diamond at the Mission. Despite their often-stated determination to win, everyone loosened up with a few beers. Of course, this was not really a factor because every team had been doing the same thing. The game itself was not particularly eventful. The Boys jumped out to a big lead, but then lost it partially because some of them would not throw the ball to the women on the team. The only drama was when one of the Boys dived for a foul ball, crashed into the backstop fence, and seriously injured himself. He was driven to hospital by one of the friends who had come along to drink beer and sit in the sun. Although everyone was concerned about his injury, they were also convinced he was just showing off for the female spectators.

When the game ended, amidst arguments about whose fault the loss was, and where the "girls" should have been allowed to play, everyone went back to the hall for a beer. After a couple more beers the loss was pretty well forgotten by all but one team member who, in everyone's opinion, was too intense about these matters. Randy got a small barbecue out of the tool box in the back of his half-ton and began to prepare his dinner. Now that they were no longer in the tournament, the Boys did not have to worry about behaving themselves and they settled into having a good time. They now concentrated on winning the team beer-drinking trophy. Every time a team member bought a beer it was recorded by the people working at the bar. At the end of the weekend the count was tallied and the team which had bought the most beer won. The trophy was three Molson Canadian beer cans on a fake marble stand with images of baseball batters made out of cheap metal and painted gold on top of the cans.

Saturday evening there was a dance in the hall. The Boys did not bother to change out of their uniforms, nor did most of the members of other teams. The hall was full and hot. Music was provided by a deejay with his own sound system. The deejay's girlfriend looked completely out of place dressed in a tight-fitting red satin dress. Everyone else in the grey cement hall wore either baseball uniforms or T-shirts and blue jeans. The girlfriend of the fellow sitting across the table from me said the deejay's girlfriend must be from out of town. Someone else said she looked like a prostitute. The beer flowed freely and when the deejay put on Van Halen's hit song "Jump" the dance area became packed with people.

Aside from partying, the Boys used the "Boogie," as these dances are referred to, to sell tickets to a benefit they were planning to hold for the wife of a deceased former team member. After he died, the Boys put his initials on the sleeves of their uniforms, and immediately began to plan the benefit for his wife. She was about three months pregnant when he passed away. At the hardware and lumber store where he worked there were no benefits or life insurance for the employees' families.

On Sunday the carnival atmosphere returned to the diamond, although it was a little more subdued since people were recovering from the night before and facing the start of the work week. Even though the Boys did not win anything for playing baseball, they generally considered the weekend to have been a success. Many tickets for the benefit were sold, and they won the team beer-drinking trophy.[14] As they lay in the back of someone's half-ton truck bantering with the outfielders of the teams in the playoff game and sipping beer, they were already planning for the next tourney weekend.

THE TRIP[15]

Going away for a tourney weekend was considered to be another highlight of the summer by the Boys. These events were planned as much as a year in advance. Once the summer arrived a team had to be assembled, entry fees collected either from the individuals or a sponsor, and transportation arranged. For this particular trip, there was a debate about whether they should rent a van and all go together or take several individual vehicles. No one wanted to have to drive because it would cut into partying time.[16] Work schedules had to be arranged, holidays booked or shifts traded with someone else, and accomodation had to be found.

A snag arose when several of the wives and girlfriends announced their desire to accompany the Boys. They were not interested in the tournament; they just wanted to get out of Thunder Bay for a couple of days and maybe do some shopping. They planned to go together in one vehicle and said they would not interfere with the Boys' fun.

Regardless of the proposed arrangements, the women's presence was one thing the Boys did not want – they were convinced it would spoil the trip. During the three weeks preceding the actual trip, a major topic of conversation was the women's desire to come along. One of the Boys, whom the others considered to be dominated by his girlfriend, was thought to be responsible for the problem. He probably wanted his girlfriend to come, they reasoned, and therefore planted the idea. At various times it was suggested that someone should inform him he was no longer welcome. As it turned out, no one ever did. The women decided not to go at the last minute and everyone was happy, at least according to the Boys.

I did not go on this trip, but I heard of it in the weeks that followed through the endless retelling of the escapades of the Boys. When they first returned from the tourney weekend in Duluth the Boys were rather quiet about their trip. Inquiries were met with a pat "Oh, it was all right." As time passed, however, the weekend became increasingly interesting, or at least the stories became funnier in the Boys' opinion.

As is true of much of the dialogue between the Boys, the verbal representation of the trip took the form of a series of anecdotal vignettes. These were told humorously as mock insults aimed at one another. There was the story of how Frank passed out in the car with his face pressed up against the window and how ugly he looked; and another about Jack having a box of beer cans split open and the cans rolling down the stairs and through the lobby of the hotel the Boys were staying in; there was the tale of how one of the Boys, getting back late to the hotel, found Chris drunk and naked in the lobby, searching for a washroom – Chris remembered none of it; there was the story about the team that won the championship and the "big fuckers" they had playing for them, including someone who had played for the Detroit Tigers; someone else had stunk up the car by vomiting in it. Finally, there was the story about the silly conversation between two of the Boys in the van on the way to the tournament. They were sitting in the back of the van and the others heard them talking about the stars they could see out the back window. One of them said, "Wow, man!" The Boys thought this expression was hilarious.

The stories were told over and over again through the remainder of the summer and came to have an evocative power. Someone would just have to say, "Wow, man" and everyone would break into hysterical laughter. "Wow, man" became the appropriate response to almost any event or comment for the rest of the summer.

All the stories had the same power. Every time they were told they appeared hilarious to the Boys who had been on the trip. They became part of the collective memory by which the Boys defined themselves. Only insiders really knew the meaning of the stories. The kind of humour was such that, as the saying goes, you had to be there. Eventually, the stories did not have to be told in their entirety. One or two appropriate words were enough to trigger laughter.

INTERPRETATIONS

As I emphasized earlier, the preceding description must be set against the serious world of work. The "sillier" aspects of the Boys' behaviour must be thought of in relation to the fact that they have been involved in wage labour since their late teenage years, and will be for their adult lives. They are in most respects normal, "responsible" citizens. The game I have described is a secular ritual, a modern local version of carnival, and like carnival it is at once legitimated by and incorporated into the hegemonic culture, and constitutes a space where themes of a culture of resistance can be played out. It thus provides a unique opportunity for grasping the nature of the tangled web of domination, subordination, and resistance in a contemporary Western capitalist society.

Sport has been seen as a ritual which mirrors society (Arens 1981), and as a means of representing society's most cherished values and instilling them in individuals (Birrell 1981). It has also been viewed as a cathartic mechanism, a way of releasing pent-up frustrations for both society and individuals. Marxist versions of the cathartic thesis interpret sport as the "bread and circuses" of the modern state, a secular "opiate of the people" (see for example Hoch 1972). Professional sport has also been interpreted as a means by which members of subordinate social classes and ethnic minorities have been able to move up the social ladder when other "normal" paths of advancement have been blocked (Reiss 1980). "Sporting countercultures" have been represented as a means of expressing opposition to the values of a dominant class. Rader (1979, 318), for example, sees prize fighting, "blood" sports, horse racing, and other "riotous" amusements in nineteenth-century Britain and the United States as a cultural reaction to repressive Victorian values (see also Donnelly 1988).

As a ritual, sport has a function similar to that of religion, especially in the secularized cultures of contemporary Western capitalist and communist nations. Professional and high-level amateur athletes often attain a status approaching the sacred. One has only to think of the reaction to the trade of Wayne Gretzky from the Edmonton Oilers to the Los Angeles Kings in August of 1988. The issue was raised both in the House of Commons in Ottawa and the provincial legislature in Edmonton. Both politicians and media personnel referred to Gretzky as a Canadian national symbol. The Gretzky trade prompted a public backlash against Peter Pocklington, owner of the Oilers, including a boycott of companies he owned and the formation of a group with the goal of purchasing the team to prevent future trades of star players. The public distress over the Ben Johnson drug scandal is an example of the society-wide angst that is experienced when the halo surrounding a star athlete is tarnished, as if a god has been revealed to be a mere mortal.

Players are important symbols, modern heroes who embody and express character traits highly valued in society. In modern Western nations (and perhaps in others as well) these include courage, perseverance, self-discipline, confidence, commitment to the team and to goals, and subordination to authority (Hargreaves 1982; Birrell 1981). The media presentation of mass spectator sporting events emphasizes these values. Talented but "undisciplined" players are the objects of scorn, while "hard workers" and "team players" are praised. One of the clearest ideological messages discernible in any sports telecast is the importance of unquestioned subordination to authority figures such as referees and coaches.

Sport also contributes to the constitution of nationalist sentiment through international competition, where the state of the nation and the legitimacy of political regimes is bound up with the performance of a country's athletes. This is evident in the fact that sport is an important aspect of foreign and domestic policy in the Soviet Union (Morton 1982), and boycotts of international sporting meets have been used by both sides in the cold war.[17]

Values such as discipline, respect for authority, and commitment are important in any form of state. Some aspects of the structure of competitive sport, however, correspond particularly well to the ideology of a capitalist mode of production. Just as one's location in the class structure is, according to the ideology, determined solely by competition in the marketplace, individuals or teams begin each match as equals, and winners and losers are determined by the skill displayed in competition – a clear representation of the principle of meritocracy upon which capitalist societies are supposedly based.

In Western capitalist nations in particular, there is also a close relationship between commercialism and sport. Corporate sponsorship of teams and leagues was and is a means of strengthening paternalistic ties between employers and employees. Prior to the Second World War, many companies in what were then Fort William and Port Arthur had teams and commonly put "star" players on the corporate payroll.[18] This practice was common in the United States and Britain as well (Wheeler 1978, 194; Reiss 1980, 300–1; Schleppi 1979). Today, professional and high-calibre amateur athletes are eagerly pursued by corporations searching for product endorsements. The sale of the exclusive right to associate corporate names with sporting events is now an important financial resource for so-called amateur sports. Even at an event such as a lob-ball tournament in Thunder Bay, the corporate presence is felt. Beer companies sponsor tournaments, providing prize money and awards such as trophies, caps, and shoulder bags. Sales representatives make the presentations at the end of the event, and the company's "community-service" vehicle is present frequently, if not constantly, during the weekend. In return for the corporate contribution to the event, only the sponsor's products are sold during the tournament.

Interpretations of sport which merely emphasize the obvious ideological elements are, however, too simplistic. They do not explain its popularity, especially for those members of society who do not belong to the dominant social groups or classes. It is one thing to recognize the way sport mirrors society; it is another to explain why large numbers of people in society are captivated by sporting events. One must ask whether the ideological messages explicitly expressed or encoded in the structure of a competitive game are passively absorbed by the viewers, or whether alternate interpretations are possible.

Sport has a compelling dramatic element. In a match, the audience sees many features of everyday life played out in dramatic form. Whether the athletes intend to play the roles or not, some are cast as villains and others as "good guys," some are underdogs while others are despised for their privileges. The roles are assigned by the spectators and the media. Fans typically love the home team and hate the visitors. The games become struggles between good and evil, between the privileged and the underprivileged, between the local and the foreign. In sport fate rules dispassionately; the outcome of a game often depends on an uncontrollable happening such as a lucky bounce. For committed fans referees' decisions are often perceived as examples of the misuse of arbitrary power, rather than the neutral exercise of authority.

Part of the appeal of sport to the masses is that, unlike official rituals and the drama of professional theatre which are controlled by the dominant groups in society, sport offers the people a chance to play a role, to participate (Hargreaves 1982, 124). One does not have to wait politely for the final curtain to express approval or disapproval. At spectator sports, the crowd is involved from the beginning, and in participatory sports average people can play roles as they see fit, not as an official script says they should. There is a populist element to sport which few other rituals have in modern society. Sport follows, in this sense, in the tradition of popular theatre and the great festivals of the Middle Ages (Hargeaves 1982, 125). Theories which interpret modern sport only as a clever diversion created by the ruling class to undermine class consciousness, do not understand that sport may also provide an avenue for the assertion of class being. Sport is a site of the class struggle over the meaning of symbols and practices (Donnelly 1988).

One must distinguish between mass spectator sports and local participatory sports. The former are under the control of the bourgeoisie and thus possess the aura of officially-sanctioned rituals. But the audience has often contested this control, erupting into the game and investing it with meaning contrary to official expectations. This is part of the rationale behind fan violence (Taylor 1982).

At another level, one must distinguish between the official presentation of a game and the way it is "read" by the spectators. Viewing a game on the television can be, and for the Boys often is, a social occasion. The Boys' interpretation of the event frequently varies considerably from that of the official commentators. "Hockey Night in Canada," a veritable Canadian institution, is, for the announcers, a weekly display during the winter months of the values mentioned earlier – commitment, courage, discipline, subordination to authority, and so on. For the Boys it is an excuse to get together, drink some beer, play cards, and talk about work. The most interesting features of the hockey game in their opinion are the events which the official commentators ignore or criticize – the fights,[19] a bad call by the referee, and the role of luck in determining the outcome. This is obviously not an expression of class consciousness in the sense of a developed theory of class relationships, but it is an assertion of popular values against official interpretations.

Local sport has been an important aspect of the constitution of working-class culture. In England, football developed as a working-class activity, and football hooliganism has been interpreted as an attempt by working-class youth to re-establish a working-class presence and control over a sport which has been commercialized and taken over by the bourgeoisie (Korr 1978; Wheeler 1978; Baker 1979; Critcher 1979; Taylor 1982).

Bryan Palmer, a labour historian, argues that popular cultural events including sports were important in the maintenance of the working-class community in Hamilton prior to World War I.

These were not insignificant or minor events, inconsequential in the grand context of class conflict or the progressive expansion of the labour movement. Baseball games, mechanics' festivals, union balls, commemorative suppers, picnics and parades formed a vital part of the very stuff of everyday life, important in their own right and too long ignored by labour historians lusting after the episodic or explicitly political. They were part of a culture that bred and conditioned solidarity, a prerequisite to any struggle attempting to better the lot of working men and women. Their continuous presence in the years 1860–1914, despite shifts in their locale and importance, lent strength to the working-class community, providing coherence and stability that had important ramifications in other realms. (Palmer 1979, 58)

Lob-ball as Signifying Practice

As a ritual, lob-ball expresses values central to the Boys' identity, both in the way the game is structured and the manner in which it is played. Some of these values are expressions of a subculture constituted in opposition to the dominant culture. Others, however, reflect ideas held throughout society and thus illustrate the extent to which hegemonic ideas have saturated the consciousness of the Boys and, by extension, the local white male working class. Lob-ball is a clear example of the way hegemony operates in the modern state. It is a ritual rebellion which is contained within dominant structures of society. From a theoretical perspective, its ultimate social meaning is ambiguous; it represents the fact that there is a partial perception among the working class of the conditions of its own existence and a response to that.

Lob-ball is a celebration of the low side of the dichotomy between high and low culture. The Boys identify with the immediate, the local, the popular in all things. Sport of the nature of lob-ball is part of low culture. High culture is considered esoteric by definition, hence élitist, and the Boys' class upbringing has prevented their exposure to the cultural codes required to enjoy it. The Boys do not read literature; they do not listen to classical music; they do not go to the theatre; ballet is boring in their opinion, and the masculinity or sexual orientation of men who are involved or interested in it is a frequent subject of gossip. Their interest in films, which is limited in any event, does not extend beyond the normal range of Hollywood productions – one of them explained to me that he was not interested in any film which required thinking since the point of going to the movies was to relax. Lob-ball is a physical activity, whereas much of high culture is intellectual. The rules of lob-ball are such that only those individuals with severe physical handicaps cannot play.[20] Serious athletes are not welcome and probably would not find the game interesting because of the relatively low level of competition involved. The Boys are interested in many team sports but not élite individual sports. They are not "jocks," a term which they use derogatorily to refer to serious athletes. Lob-ball is, therefore, accessible to anyone. It is a populist game.

The structure of the teams is also populist. They are formed on the most flexible basis – friendship. There are no competitive tryouts and everyone plays. There is an attempt to ensure that everyone has equal playing time, or at least is satisfied with the amount of time he plays.

Lob-ball, like all team sports, is a group activity. This was a major factor in the Boys' explanations of their own interest in the game and in the importance of team uniforms. When I asked them why they liked lob-ball they all mentioned the importance of being part of a group: "It's fun and you're with other people. It's better than being at home by yourself." Similarly, "It's good to get out and do things with other people. It makes you feel like you are part of something." As another put it, "I think it is important to be part of a group. The uniforms make you feel like that. I feel sorry for people that don't have friends and can't do things like this. Besides it's a laugh [laughing], these jerks are always doing something funny." The father of one of the Boys who acted as the "coach"[21] compared belonging to the lob-ball team to his military experience in World War II. Like the Boys he felt that everyone had a need to belong to a group. For his generation the war fulfilled that need because everyone joined the armed forces. He compared the behaviour of the Boys to that of his squadron in the air force. Just as the Boys visited the bar after each game, the squadron's patrol flights were always followed by a trip to the pub. I asked him if the war was not actually about politics and ideology, and if these were not the reasons why he had volunteered. As he recounted it, his volunteering had little to do with the fight against fascism because that did not really mean much to him at the time. He and a friend went for a beer after work one day and decided they would sign up. "Everyone was doing it and it seemed kind of exciting."[22]

The uniforms were and are, according to the coach, a very important element in the appeal of both joining the armed forces and of belonging to the lob-ball team. When I joined the team in the summer of 1985, I did not initially have a uniform and I was reluctant to spend the seventy or eighty dollars that a new uniform cost. Without my requesting it, one of the Boys contacted someone who had been on the team two years before and arranged for him to sell me his uniform for twenty-five dollars. When I arrived for the first time wearing the uniform, everyone commented on my appearance. Later, over beers by the back of someone's half-ton truck, I asked why the uniform was so important. One of them answered that "it just makes you feel better, you feel like you're part of the team." As so often happened, many of the others met my questions with a look of exasperation. Was I really so dumb that I had to ask?

Within the informal group of the team, generalized reciprocity reigns supreme. No one asks who has or has not contributed to the team's beer fund. It is assumed that everyone contributes his share. In the bar after the game, everyone takes turns buying rounds. If someone is short of money one evening someone else or several other people stand him drinks. This "just happens"; one does not need to ask. Of course, the gift does contain an obligation. Everyone is expected to behave in the same manner. Anyone who is perceived to be too concerned with money, about who has paid for what, is the object of scorn. True friends, for the Boys, are people who give to each other without asking, and this extends beyond the walls of the bar after a game.

I stated earlier that there is an interesting correspondence between the competitive element of sport and the competitive features of a capitalist mode of production. Lob-ball, at least the way it is played in the the Boys' league, de-emphasizes the competitive nature of the game. The Boys do like to win, as do the other teams in the league, but competitiveness is tempered by the overriding principle of fun. It must not destroy the group and anyone who takes the game too seriously is sneered at. The object of the game is to have fun and anything that might jeopardize this result is shunned.

The importance of fun as a goal of the Boys' leisure should not be underestimated. My own interest in analyzing their leisure was a source of bewilderment and even exasperation to them. "Christ, you take something that is a laugh and make it sound so boring." Other versions of this theme were stated frequently. Of course, the search for pleasure, for a laugh, is not unique to them, or to the working class as a whole. But against the seriousness of the world of work, the civilities of bourgeois society, and the melancholy of Western Marxism which pretends to speak for the working class, the importance of the laugh to people like the Boys takes on a symbolic significance.[23] An insistence on having fun is not simple escapism, nor is it merely a surrender to the hedonistic impulse of contemporary society, although neither of these elements can be left out of account. The insistence on having fun is also an affirmation that the point of work should be the enjoyment of life, rather than production for its own sake. Enjoyment denied in the labour process becomes an obsession in the realm of leisure.

In the activities surrounding the game, and especially during tournaments, the carnivalesque spirit is evident. Bodily style emphasizes openness and release. Much of the humour relates to what Bakhtin (1984, 368–436) calls the "material bodily lower stratum." Penises, arses, excretion, vomiting, and farting are the subject of endless humorous commentary. Scatalogical and other such images are also used discursively to level hierarchical distinctions. Sayings such as "He's so stuck-up he thinks his shit doesn't stink" operate by juxtaposing a social distinction with the basest human bodily functions which render us all equal.

Excessive consumption leads to excessive release – vomiting, farting, belching – all of which is turned into a joke. The emphasis on release contrasts with the importance of self-control in middle-class culture: "Release is the antithesis of discipline, a disengagement or extrication from imposed and internalized controls. Instead of a language of will power and regulation, there exists a language of well-being, contentment and enjoyment ... In the absence of a capacity to control one's life situation, more characteristic of working-class experience, what is important is to have another attitude toward it, a positive and easy-going attitude" (Crawford 1984, 81–2). The activities surrounding lob-ball symbolically invert dominant ideas about self-control, discipline, and fun.

Despite the lack of emphasis on competitiveness, the games are still dramatic. Usually, many runs are scored and games often have a seesaw flow. One team will score a large number of runs, only to see its lead disappear when its opponents come to bat. Because of the quality of the field and the skill levels of the players nothing can be taken for granted. There are no routine flyballs or groundballs in these games because one is never certain that the ball will not take a strange bounce or that the outfielder will not trip and fall down, and even if no accidents befall the players, the play may not be completed because of a lack of skill. In many respects these games are more exciting and more fun than professional baseball games because mistakes and accidents are relatively rare at higher levels of play. Plays become routine and therefore hold less dramatic potential. Fate truly does rule at lob-ball matches and no one is in a hurry to try and change this through practice or training.

In all these ways, lob-ball is a means by which the Boys differentiate themselves from the dominant values they encounter in their work and in other areas of life, such as their interaction with government bureaucracy. In the dominant culture, especially at the tail-end of the twentieth century, there is a strong moralistic and puritanical streak; the Boys celebrate fun. In the labour market they are individuated; in their leisure time they seek group activities. In everyday life they are buffeted by economic forces and authoritarian structures; through the lob-ball team they emphasize human interpersonal relations based on friendship rather than necessity. The formal and impersonal principles of market exchange rule in the larger world; the group emphasizes generalized reciprocity. Lob-ball is a signifying practice through which the Boys try to construct a different world based on cultural themes denied in the dominant discourse and economic structures in which they are imprisoned.

Lob-ball and Social Reproduction:
Consumerism

Lob-ball is ritual rebellion on a minor scale, but it is contained within clear economic and ideological structures. One of the marks of modern capitalist societies is the development of the "culture industry" (Adorno and Horkheimer 1979, 120–67). Leisure has in many respects become a commodity. One purchases fun in the marketplace, one no longer creates it out of self-produced use values. This is a logical development of capital's ongoing search for a means of valorization. As it searches out new investment opportunities and new markets it penetrates regions of the world and parts of society previously untouched by the capitalist mode of production.

This is a double-edged process. On the one hand, it tends to separate consumers from producers. Critics fear the decline of cultural standards as cultural objects are aimed at the lowest common denominator so as to generate a mass market, and the destruction of unique cultural practices (Adorno and Horkheimer 1979, 120–67; Hoggart 1957). People become passive consumers of culture rather than producers. The bourgeoisie spoon-feeds a thin cultural gruel to a complacent, individuated population and furthers the aims of capital in the process. Critical analyses of modern spectator sport are an extension of this logic to the area of sport. On the other hand, mass production does make cultural products available to more people than was the case in the past. Modern printing techniques, for example, make it possible for greater numbers of people to read the classics, since they can be produced more cheaply and in larger quantity.

Modern sport has created a mass market for certain products, whether they be professional baseball games or baseball gloves. The Boys do spend a large amount of money on lob-ball and the game is suffused with commercialism, from the purchase of equipment and beer to the sponsorship of teams, leagues, and tournaments by local and national businesses. In this sense, even though one can read lob-ball as a ritual expression of resistance to dominant economic and ideological features of the social formation in which the Boys live, it is enmeshed in a thoroughly capitalistic set of structures. The system is in no way undermined by the Boys' activity.

Lob-ball and the Reproduction of Gendered Identities

One of the most marked features of lob-ball and the activities surrounding it is the way gender divisions are expressed and reproduced. In its various meanings and social functions male bonding is one of the most important of these expressions. Male bonding, insofar as it is about men forming relations with other men, does not in and of itself stand in necessary contradiction with the themes of resistance which resonate through the lob-ball games and tournaments. To the extent that the game and the activities associated with it emphasize the social as opposed to the individual, male bonding is just a specific example of how a social group can be constituted in a society which is highly individuated. But male bonding, in this context at least, is part of the expression and reproduction of masculinity, and as such is an aspect of the constitution and reproduction of gendered identities and the social relations this entails. The Boys are, therefore, imprisoned in an ideological web which marks one of the limits of the liberating potential of the activities I have been describing.

Paradoxically, masculinity is expressed most strongly in the endless series of jokes and innuendoes regarding homosexuality. The sexual orientation of individuals is an endless topic of commentary, much of it humorous, but, like so much humour, it has a dark underside. I have already indicated that men who, from the Boys' perspective, are overly interested in some element of so-called high culture are suspected of homosexuality. Of course, the Boys are merely espousing a widespread stereotype. Body and clothing styles are scrutinized for signs of homosexuality. A man who is too well groomed is a potential homosexual as is any man who is overly emotional in public. "He's a fag"; "You are a goddamn faggot" – these are among the most common insults the Boys use. They are equally alert to what in their minds are signs of lesbianism, again identified on the basis of body language and clothing style.

Jokes with one another which have homosexual overtones invert the Boys' own apparent obsession with heterosexuality, and thus drive home the significance of heterosexuality as an aspect of masculinity. They are also part of the carnivalesque atmosphere that reigns, especially on tourney weekends. They signify close friendship, for only with one's closest friends can one joke about such matters. Fear of being labelled homosexual, or at least of having your masculinity questioned, means that such horseplay can only take place within a context where one's masculinity is beyond doubt.

One of the most striking elements of the Boys' culture as expressed in the game is the way women are excluded, or their role strongly circumscribed. Women are included in the games but only in a supportive role. Their function corresponds to the role they play in domestic production. Just as women support male labourers by producing meals, clean clothes, and a comfortable environment in which to relax, and see to male emotional and sexual needs, at the lob-ball games they act as fans, as drivers if their mate drinks too much, and as providers of clean uniforms and food. It is not an exaggeration to say that a woman's primary role in this ritual is to ensure that her man enjoys himself. In the bar after the games, the table normally divides into two halves, one for the women and one for the men. The latter generally carry on their conversations as if the women were not present. Once in a while, if the jokes become too crude, someone might say, "Hey, there's women present, take it easy." As often as not such an intervention is met with a laugh and a barrage of rude comments. The women sit at their end of the table, quietly talking among themselves.

Language can be used to define social and cultural space. The abundant use of foul language is a means of symbolically expressing the fact that the game, the field, the back of the half-ton, and the bar are all male spaces. "Fuck" is employed as verb, subject, adjective, and adverb. It can appear in all these roles in the same statement. Bars are no longer off limits to women, but they are still male public spaces (Hey 1986), and that space is defended through language. It is the language of the shopfloor transferred to the leisure sphere.

The stereotype of the male breadwinner is changing in the face of women's struggles to gain access to what were traditionally male jobs (Livingstone and Luxton 1989). But the image of the workplace as a masculine domain persists, especially in large industrial enterprises. Paper mills, bush camps, mines, railways, grain elevators, construction projects – the ideal work places for many working-class men in northwestern Ontario – have historically been the preserve of men. The boredom and alienation of this kind of wage labour is overcome by interpreting it as a test of masculinity. Workers prove their worth as men by their ability to withstand dirt, noise, danger, and boredom. Working conditions are "read" as a challenge to masculinity, rather than as an expression of the exploitation of capitalist relations of production. "Discontent with work is turned away from a political discontent and confused in its logic by a huge detour into the symbolic" (Willis 1979, 196).

Stan Gray has argued that the workplace is a last sanctum of the male culture, a world where men

could get away from the world of women, away from responsibility and children and civilized society's cultural restraints. In the plant they could revel in the rough and tumble of a masculine world of physical harshness, of constant swearing and rough behaviour, of half-serious fighting and competition with each other and more serious fighting with the boss. It was eight hours full of filth and dirt and grease and grime and sweat – manual labour and a manly atmosphere. They could be vulgar and obscene, talk about football and car repairs, and let their hair down. Boys could be boys. (Gray 1987, 225)

Like the men at Gray's electronics factory trying to protect the shop-floor from the presence of women, the Boys try to preserve a male world by excluding women. They do this through explicit acts of exclusion, and through the symbolic defence of male cultural space. The women who come along are tolerated. Although they are certainly needed, there is little explicit attempt to accommodate them or their wishes.

Masculinity is in part expressed through control over women. Having a "girlfriend" or wife who comes to the game, sits quietly, does not complain, does not get upset about the amount one drinks afterwards, is an indication of one's control over her. Of course, in practice the women are not passive and submissive creatures, and this frequently generates problems. Arguments between the Boy's and their wives or partners were not uncommon. Two of the Boys had already been through marriages, and the long-term relationships of two others came apart during the two years of my field work.

The "pull of the male clique" creates problems for relationships. The women do have the unenviable task of being the guardians of the collective welfare of the couple and family, or future family. They are the ones who must discourage their husbands or male partners from having one more beer, remind them that tomorrow is a work day, or, if they have children, that the children are at the babysitter's. Many women tire of this role, or refuse to play it at all.

The men are friends. Many of the women had never met until they accompanied the Boys to one of their activities. The women's presence at the activities of the informal group is dependent upon their male partners and they relate to the group as a whole, including the other women, through them.

Women who have grown up in cities or towns such as those in Northwestern Ontario are socialized into a supportive role regarding the world of sports and male leisure. In all the households I know, including the one I grew up in, the domestic routine is adjusted to fit the requirements of the son's or husband's leisure schedule. Mothers with outside jobs rush home to prepare a quick meal so the son or husband can make it to an early evening game. At Tom Thumb and Peewee hockey games, gender divisions are clearly marked. The mothers and wives sit together and noisily cheer for their son's team. The fathers sit, or frequently stand, together in another part of the rink. Since the expression of too much emotion is considered unmanly, they are quieter than the women, and whereas the latter lend ardent emotional support to "their" team, the fathers discuss technical aspects of the game such as the merit of various players and team strategy. Emotional displays from the men usually involve someone "losing it" and erupting in vicious verbal abuse of a referee, coach, or even one of the players. The young boys are on the ice. Among the youngest players – those in the Atom or Tom Thumb divisions – many have yet to develop rudimentary hockey skills, but they all know the appropriate ritual response to any given situation. The young girls run around the rink in small packs hounding their mothers for money for chips, pop, and chocolate bars. The adults' attention is focused on the young boys and the game they play. A "good" daughter is one who does not annoy her mother (generally they do not approach their fathers at a game) by demanding too much attention. These young girls grow up knowing that male leisure comes first, especially in sports.

Although cohabitation outside of marriage is common, marriage is still the norm in the Boys' world.[24] Sexual morality is looser, perhaps, than it was in their parents' generation; yet the roles of males and females have not changed greatly. Women are still the "homemakers." As I indicated in chapter 3, the employment opportunities for women in Thunder Bay are somewhat more limited than in the province as a whole. All the girlfriends and wives worked in clerical or retail jobs, except for two who were university students.[25] None of them earned a higher salary than their boyfriends and none, other than the two students, were planning a career.

In the stories the Boys tell, they still clearly distinguish between the kind of women they would live with and hope to marry, and those with whom one might "have a good time" for an evening or weekend. In this sense, the "madonna/whore" dichotomy remains a powerful element of the Boys' image of women.

As was abundantly evident during the tourney weekend, women are assumed to be incapable, or at least less capable, of performing what are considered male activities such as sport. Of course, to an extent this is true because the women have rarely been invited to participate and have therefore rarely had the chance to develop even the (in many cases) minimal skills of the men. Given the nature of lob-ball and the skill levels required, it is difficult to imagine that anyone, male or female, is incapable of playing. This division is simply a reflection of the ideological construction of the female as a lesser other.

In their treatment of women, the Boys are reproducing the system of inequality based upon gender which crosses all social classes. It would be wrong, however, to conclude from this that class does not matter. Working-class men certainly do contribute to the maintenance of a system of patriarchy which subordinates women. Yet bourgeois women can dominate working-class men. Carrigan, Connell, and Lee argue that one of the central facts about patriarchy in the contemporary capitalist world is that "men in general are advantaged through the subordination of women." They quickly point out, however, that "men in general" is a problematic concept, and that the "intersections of gender relations with class and race relations yield many other situations where rich white heterosexual women, for instance, are employers of working-class men, patrons of homosexual men, or politically dominant over black men" (1987, 177). As they go on to say, it would be "crass" to argue that this means women are "not subordinated in general." The point is rather that within the hegemonic patriarchal system there are a variety of masculinities.

Many commentators have pointed out that, while gender inequality is to be found in all social classes, it manifests itself in somewhat different forms. The exclusion of women from the world of men is stronger in the working class. As commentators on the working-class family have pointed out, there is frequently a major communication problem between husbands and wives. The male worker's valuation of physical and emotional toughness means that men do not think it is appropriate to talk to their spouses about work. Real men do not "whine" or "gripe" about their situation. Of course, the image of women as technically incompetent also means that it is assumed women will not be able to understand what happens at work (Komarovsky 1967, 148–55). The strong separation between home and work is also a separation of men and women. This contrasts with the role that the wives of professional men play in their husbands' careers. Entertaining business clients, partners, or colleagues is part of the job, and wives are deeply involved in this. Their role is to be a good entertainer, someone who is skilled at putting on a dinner party, someone who is a good conversationalist. They are, therefore, not excluded from the male world of work so much as included in a subordinate role. Rubin poses the question whether there is such a great difference in relations between the sexes in the working class and the middle class. Her answer is that it is not *too* different, but there is less fragmentation of work and leisure among the middle class. "For the professional the fragmentation ... doesn't exist. Work and life – which also means play – are part and parcel of each other. Their friends are often colleagues or other professionals in similar or related fields. Evenings spent with them mean that the ideas that engage them at work also involve them at play. Social life is almost always a coupled affair, a shared experience of husband and wife" (Rubin 1976, 190).

To read this passage from a different angle, what it draws attention to is that the way middle-class men express their masculinity is different, perhaps not too different, but different nonetheless from the way working-class men do the same thing. Thus, class matters, and for the Boys and the other workers I know, it is impossible to separate their ideas about masculinity and femininity from their ideas about their work and play.

Lob-ball, viewed as a ritual text, illustrates both the potential and limits of the development of class consciousness among the Boys and, by extension, the local male white working class. Raymond Williams has written that "what is properly meant by 'working class culture'" is "the basic collective idea, and the institutions, manners, habits of thought, and intentions which proceed from this" (1963, 313). He contrasts this with bourgeois culture defined by the "basic individualist idea." Lob-ball is an expression of the social as opposed to the individual emphasis in the Boys' culture. But the basic collective idea that underlies their culture is enclosed within economic and ideological structures which render it a defensive reaction against the wider world rather than an opening into a possible future.

CHAPTER FIVE

Race, Ethnicity, and Regionalism in Working-Class Culture

Racism is not dealt with as a general feature of human societies, but with historically-specific racisms. Beginning with an assumption of difference, of specificity rather than a unitary, trans-historical or universal "structure." This is not to deny that there might well be discovered to be certain common features to all those social systems to which one would wish to attribute the designation, "racially structured." But ... such a general theory of racism is not the most favourable source for theoretical development and investigation ... This is a warning against extrapolating a common and universal structure to racism, which remains essentially the same, outside of its specific historical location.

(Stuart Hall 1980, 336–7)

INTRODUCTION

Racial and ethnic characteristics are powerful symbols in the myths which the Boys adopt to explain their own and others' place in a perceived set of power relations. From an anthropological perspective the concept of "race" has no analytical or scientific value. I use the term here only because human physical characteristics, even if they are often inextricably bound up with phenomena which are cultural in origin, are important symbols in the classificatory schemes of my informants. I should add that these are *perceived* physical differences. On closer and more critical inspection they may not actually have much substance. But as long as people perceive them to exist, and act and think on that basis, they have real material effects.

There is a literature on the difference between race and ethnicity as forms of identity. The differences are important, but in the present context, they are not particularly relevant. In the cultural world under investigation here, the distinctions academics make are of no interest. The line between cultural and biological differences is unclear. Categories such as white and Indian are formed according to different principles than categories such as Italian and English. One does refer principally to physical characteristics, whereas the other is based upon country of origin and culture. But in the everyday world, when people make these distinctions, it is usually a combination of physical and cultural markers that are used. One evening while discussing the people at another table in the bar, someone said, "They must be Italian." "How do you know that?" I inquired. "Just look at them" was the response. Upon further discussion, it became clear that what I was supposed to see was both their physical appearance, such as relatively dark skin and curly hair, and cultural factors, such as the excited nature of the conversation that was taking place. In many other contexts, when discussions of Indians arose, the same combination of physical and cultural characteristics were used to identify the racial and ethnic origin of the individuals under discussion. Physical markers such as relatively dark skin, straight black hair, high cheekbones, and so on become significant in relation to a cultural, social, and economic context. It is in this sense that the intellectual arguments about what are racial and what are ethnic phenomena are irrelevant here.

In the previous chapter, using lob-ball as an example, I showed how the Boys express resistance to their subordinate position in the relations of production and how their resistance is refracted through consumerism and sexism. The "Indian" is employed as a symbol through which the Boys establish their own moral worth and their difference from the perceived dominant power bloc. They "imagine" their own community in opposition to others (Anderson 1984, 15), and racial and ethnic characteristics provide easily discernible markers upon which such divisions can be constituted.

Berkhofer, in his study of the image of the Indian in white culture, points out the ideological nature of the term Indian: "Since the original inhabitants of the Western Hemisphere neither called themselves by a single term nor understood themselves as a collectivity, the idea and image of the Indian must be a White conception. Native Americans were and are real, but the *Indian* was a White invention and still remains largely a White image, if not stereotype" (Berkhofer 1979, 3; emphasis in original).

For the Boys, and for many white people in Thunder Bay and in northwestern Ontario as a whole, the most important racial and ethnic distinction today is between whites and Indians. The Indian is perceived as an inferior other against whom whites define themselves. The Indian is also a powerful symbol in the whites' understanding of their relationship to other whites, especially those in the metropolis located in the southern part of the province. The Indian thus plays a symbolic role in two sets of relationships, one between local whites and local Natives, and the other between local whites and other whites. Ironically, Natives, who are clearly at the bottom of the local social hierarchy in both material and ideological terms, have become symbols of the domination of local whites by the external white power bloc. The Indian is both the object of derision and the object of envy for the local whites. The least powerful segment of local society has come to represent local white powerlessness. The whites' understanding of their own subordinate position in the broader society is refracted into a racist perspective against Native people.

RACE AND ETHNICITY AMONG PEOPLE OF EUROPEAN ANCESTRY IN THUNDER BAY

Today, race and ethnicity are not significant social markers between people of European ancestry in Thunder Bay, at least in terms of the local social hierarchy. But in the recent past a person's racial or ethnic affiliation often denoted a place in the hierarchies of occupation, residence, and social class.[1] The working class was fractured along ethnic lines and the division of labour between industries was to a large extent based on ethnicity. The popular local version of this historic situation is as follows: the railroad was an English preserve; Finns and French Canadians composed a large portion of the labour force in the forest industry; construction work was an Italian activity; and Eastern Europeans worked the freight sheds and performed other kinds of heavy manual work.

This characterization of the ethnic division of labour reflects the stereotypes attached to different ethnic groups as much as it describes the actual historical situation. Not all Finns and French Canadians were lumberjacks and there were British unskilled labourers in the freight sheds alongside Italians and Ukrainians. Nonetheless, ethnicity was a significant factor in the social, economic, and political divisions in the city and within the working class.

In 1913, the Department of Temperance and Moral Reform of the Methodist Church and the Board of Social Service and Evangelism of the Presbyterian Church directed a "Preliminary and General Social Survey" of Fort William and Port Arthur. The moral and religious life of non-Anglo-Saxon immigrants was of central concern to officials of both churches. Of Fort William the report states:

There may be said to be three distinct grades of society: The more well-to-do, living in the better residential quarters, who have made a competence from real-estate investments; the Artisan class consisting mainly of English-speaking people, who have come to provide the skilled labour for the City's numerous industries; and the ever-increasing horde of unskilled workers: Ruthenians, Russians, Italians, and many others who do the railway construction work and the rough labour and freight handling about the factories and docks. (Stewart 1913a, 10)

In Port Arthur, "the steady encroachment of the immigrant people [was] not so marked" but the life of the city was said to have "a decidedly Finnish cast" (Stewart 1913b, 5): "Like Fort William, the population readily falls into 3 classes: The wealthy class of early settlers, who have grown up in the City, and the business and professional men; the Artisans or skilled labor class; the non-English-speaking immigrant population, among whom the Finns constitute the aristocracy, and are the link connecting the immigrant with the Artisan class" (Stewart 1913b, 5).

In the decade 1901–11 the population of Thunder Bay District increased by 252 per cent, the second highest expansion in the country (Dominion Bureau of Statistics 1936, 124). This population explosion was largely the result of immigration which included large numbers of people from eastern and southern Europe. In 1911 over twenty-four per cent of the Fort William population was born in "foreign countries," meaning for the most part continental Europe, since only three per cent of the foreign-born came from the United States (Dominion Bureau of Statistics 1913, 447). The social survey directed by the Methodist and Presbyterian churches in 1913 stated on the basis of official statistics that one-third of the population was neither Canadian, English, Irish, Scottish, nor American. The author of the report did not trust these figures: "We have no doubt that there is a far greater proportion of non-Anglo-Saxons" (Stewart 1913a, 7). Evidence to support this statement came from a house-by-house survey conducted on two blocks of the coal-docks section and one block in Westfort, both areas where immigrants lived.

Census data for Port Arthur reveal a similar pattern. More than twenty-two per cent of the population was born in "foreign countries." Indeed, in 1911 Fort William and Port Arthur had the highest percentage of foreign-born inhabitants of the sixty-four Canadian cities with populations greater than seven thousand (Dominion Bureau of Statistics 1913, 447).

For the self-appointed guardians of community morality the presence of these foreigners was a grave concern. It appeared that they lived and worked within their own communities and were therefore immune to the influences of Canadian life. Children were taught English in school but adults had little contact with the larger environment. In Fort William, the

social, political and industrial forces in the community are having little force in the Canadianization of these peoples in as far as the adults are concerned at least ... They attend their own churches ... They have their own societies and their own social gatherings. The English papers scarcely reach them at all, such reading as they do generally being in their own native papers. In the industries, they work in their own national groups to a very great extent, this being true of the foundries and all the railroad construction work, so that they come into little contact with Canadian life. (Stewart 1913a, 8)

A similar situation prevailed in Port Arthur.

The immigrants to a certain extent form a City within a City. They are not reached by the English Canadian papers to any appreciable extent, and very few of them speak English ... Several of the immigrants have their own churches, and these to a considerable degree prevent their Canadianization ... There are different national societies among them, and the Finns have their socialist society, and these serve to perpetuate old world conditions in a New Ontario City. The Industrial associations do not serve to Canadianize to any marked degree because the immigrants work in groups and even in industry maintain a life of their own. (Stewart 1913b, 4)

In the years prior to World War I, "foreigners" played a leading role in a series of violent strikes and demonstrations against the railroad companies (Morrison 1974, 1976). The companies were able to exploit ethnic divisions among workers to break the strikes and prevent the formation of unions. Local newspapers focused on the danger to the Anglo-Saxon community and to British values posed by large numbers of unassimilated immigrants from southern and eastern Europe, and investigative journalists looked into the sanitary, social, and moral conditions of the "Latin races" in the cities (*Daily Times-Journal* 21 August 1909, 1). They drew a strong connection between the use of violence and the immigrants, and played upon the fears of the local Anglo-Saxon community (MacDonald 1976). Not only were the newcomers not acculturated to peaceful labour tactics such as those practised by British trade unionists but they also brought "dangerous" socialist ideas with them from their homelands.

The Finns and eastern Europeans came from the Tsarist and Austro-Hungarian empires. Many of the Finns had come to Canada in the wake of the failed 1905 revolution, while others, who were social democrats and fought with the Reds after the 1917 revolution, had to leave when the Whites won the post-revolution civil war in Finland. Finns were very active in both the national and local socialist and communist movements. One of the stated goals of the Finnish Organization of Canada was the furtherance of the labour movement as a whole. It was outlawed by the Canadian government in 1940 (Pilli 1981; Eklund 1981; Radforth 1981, 1987, 107–58). Many Ukrainians were also active in the local labour movement and built a Labour Temple in the east end of Fort William in 1928. Although Italians and Greeks played an important part in the labour "troubles" in Fort William and Port Arthur and were victims of anti-immigrant fears throughout the country, socialist politics do not seem to have been as central a feature of their culture (Pucci 1978).

In the post-war era, ethnicity has declined as a source and justification of social inequality among people of European ancestry. The major influx of non-British European immigrants took place prior to the Second World War. The offspring of the early waves of immigrants were educated in Canada and socialized into the predominant culture. For groups like the Finns, integration began in the interwar years as they moved out of the Finnish ghetto and into more skilled jobs (Tolvanen 1981).

The elevators had been a Scottish preserve in the early years of their existence. By the mid-1970s this was no longer the case. In the grain elevator where I worked in 1974–75, a wide spectrum of ethnic groups were represented. Among the eighteen workers in the track shed, there were six British, two Finns, two French Canadians, two Ukrainians, two Italians, one Pole, one Dane, one Native (Mohawk), and one person who always claimed not to know his ethnic heritage. The foreman and supervisor were British, and the elevator superintendent was Greek.[2]

Ethnicity among whites is important to the Boys only as a source of jokes, and these are endless. Jokes about Finns revolve around the idea that they drink a lot. Eastern Europeans are ridiculed for their supposed lack of intelligence. Italians are stereotyped as extremely emotional.

The Boys are descended from a number of different European ethnic groups. They joked continuously with one another about such things, but ethnicity was not considered an important enough issue to disqualify someone from group membership. European ethnicity does not play a role in their selection of female companions. The Boys who are not of British descent are "name" ethnics, to employ Stymeist's terminology (1975, 54), and their ethnic heritage carries little social significance, at least in terms of employment, class, or social status.[3]

THE IMAGE OF THE INDIAN IN CONTEMPORARY THUNDER BAY

Racial and ethnic differences are not, however, a non-issue in contemporary Thunder Bay. Native people are the one group for whom biological and cultural ancestry is a stigma with important social ramifications.

The Boys do not have a developed theory of white superiority. Their prejudices are not the product of formalized justifications for white dominance over Native people. They do not perceive themselves as dominant over anyone, but rather as the victims of a system which has mis-identified the true sources of social inequality. Their racism is rooted in the immediate experience of their everyday lives and in the prejudices and practices which are widely present in the culture of the Anglo-Saxon world.

Although their ideas about Natives are not straightforward, or always negative, the image of the Indian which appears most frequently in the Boys' discourse is generally derogatory. In jokes, off-hand comments, and general banter and gossip, the Indian stands for negative personality traits. An individual is often denigrated by the suggestion that only Indians would find him or her attractive. Behaviour that is considered outrageous is referred to as "going Indian." This involves a variety of activities – excessive drinking, fighting, vandalism, or just conducting oneself in a rude or obnoxious manner. The idea of the Indian as the living embodiment of pathological behavioural characteristics is never far from the surface of the mind or the tip of the tongue. A story about a rude drunk in a public place automatically generates a comment such as "An Indian, eh?" Misbehaviour on the part of a group of high-school students is explained with the observation "that they were probably all Indians." Vandalism of new cars in an automobile sales lot is accounted for by the "fact" that "lots of Indians live around there." These are just a few examples from a vast repertoire of behaviours which are considered typical of Indians.

In the preceding chapter I referred to the destruction of the baseball diamond where the Boys play, and their conviction that

Indians were responsible for it. It was, for them, so obvious as to be beyond doubt. I personally do not know who was responsible, but it does not matter; we are dealing with a discourse which produces "truth effects."[4] The reserve is nearby; the Indians were angry because they did not have a team in the league; and this was the sort of thing Indians would do. No one was caught, but everyone was convinced they knew who was responsible. Once, when discussing the vandalism, one of the Boys suggested that a forty-ounce bottle of whisky be left at the diamond every weekend. "When they see that they'll get so excited, they'll drink it and pass out. Then we won't have to worry."

The "obviousness" of the evidence was predetermined by the stereotypes about Indians which are central to the Boys' culture. In this case there were other possible explanations of the vandalism. There is a trailer court nearby; the diamond is very close to the city and is easily accessible by car; the local Band was approached about entering a team in the league but showed no interest – none of these facts in any way threatened the "obviousness" of the explanation adopted by those who played in the league. On the contrary, their explanation triggered a new set of sarcastic comments. Arriving at the diamond on Monday evening the team discovered that the bleachers had been burned. They reckoned the Indians had had a barbecue on the weekend.

The vandalism of the baseball field generated endless commentary among the informal group. My own skepticism about their view was a portentous sign of my own difference. Critical comments on the subject initiated an uncomfortable silence at the table, a change of topic – signs that a "non-believer" was in their midst.

Indians were the one ethnic group the Boys tried to avoid. "Indian bars," drinking establishments with a large Native clientele, were shunned because of the presence of Indians. This was explicit: "There's no way I'm going in [to a well-known "Indian bar"]. Some buck is liable to stick a knife in my back. People are always getting stabbed there." Again, "You have to be tough to hang around Moccassin Square Gardens [the local nickname for another bar frequented by Natives]. You're going to wake up on the railroad tracks with all your money gone."

I visited the "Indian bars" on average once a week during the first year of my fieldwork. Several of the Boys warned me that this was not a wise thing to do. They told me that a "squaw" was going to try and pick me up and "then the whole tribe is going to be out to get you." One of them said, laughingly, that I must like my meat smoked, a suggestion that I was interested in Native women as sexual partners. Whites who frequent "Indian bars" are considered to be "losers."

Native women were the only women with whom the Boys would not mix. People who lived with or married Natives were thought to be "hard up," that is, incapable of having a relationship with a white. A mixed Native/white couple is inevitably the subject of gossip. Native women are perceived to be "easy" or "loose." They fall as a group into the whore category of the "madonna/whore" dichotomy. If someone goes "slumming" one evening they might "pick up" a "squaw," but long-term relationships with Native women are never contemplated.

People were very willing to talk about Indians. The following conversation is typical of many I had. It took place in a bar on a cold night in January 1985.

Six of us went for beer after playing "boot hockey" on an outdoor rink. We met a couple of other friends at the bar. In the course of conversation the topic of Indians came up and I pursued the chance to question the Boys who were present about their attitudes. Fred, a forest-fire fighter, was more than happy to give me his opinion. "So you want to hear about Indians," he began.

Fred was vehement. He said that in one community he knew, "an Indian never cuts more than one day's worth of firewood. You want to know why? If he cuts any more than what he needs everybody else comes and takes it. That's the way Indians are. There are no laws up there. If you have trouble with someone you get your gun. That's the way they do it."

I unwisely interrupted at this point and said, "Maybe it's just reciprocity."

"What the fuck is that?"

"Maybe what you call stealing is really sharing. The guy who comes and takes the wood is a brother or relative of some kind, and the fellow who cut the firewood takes something from him at another time."

"Maybe," Fred replied, "but we give them too much. Up at [the community] there is a brand-new community centre built with a Wintario [a provincial lottery] grant. It cost about $300,000. It's only worth $100,000 but it is so expensive to ship everything up there. Well, you should see it now. All the windows are broken. There are shotgun blasts through the ceiling. And right on the door there is this big sign: 'This project was undertaken with a grant from Wintario.' Fuck, it's like that everywhere." Fred named another community. "Everything is new. They're driving Cadillacs."

Again I interjected. "I doubt they were given a Wintario grant to buy Cadillacs."

Sam, the other fire-fighter, commented at this point. "I think it's just that we give them too much. Things they don't want. They just want to be left alone. They like how they live."

Fred resumed. "Anyway, it's not white attitudes about Indians. What about what they think of us. They're [the government] building a new runway [at the first community he had mentioned] for their health services. Not one Indian works on the project. It's all white guys. They live in brand-new trailers. They got a satellite dish. Everything is new. The Indians hate those fuckers, man [giving the finger as he said this]. But they [the Indians] don't care. The fucking lakes up there are dead. The commercial fishermen have killed them. There is a lake about a hundred miles north of Sioux Lookout [i.e., it is isolated] and there is not a fucking fish in it."

At this point Fred stood up and walked to the washroom shaking his head. Apparently, the conversation upset him for he did not come back to our table, but went and sat at the bar with some other friends who were watching a rock video channel on the television.

Sam spoke up again. "They speak another language, you know. You should see when you work with them on a fire. I'm the white guy, the boss. You ask them to do something and they smile at you. Then they start talking in their own language. They do the work, but you always get the feeling really they're saying to each other, fuck you, pal. I don't know. Maybe it's just the language."

Fred returned. Standing over the table, he said, "Don't get me wrong, eh. There are lots of good Indians. Right now I've got four young Indian guys on my crew. They're the best workers there. It's like when they're off the reserve working a fire or something they're okay, you know. I work with Indians all the time and they're great. The smoke and bugs and shit like that doesn't bother them. Not like white guys. But when they go back to the reserve they get all fucked up."

A brief silence settled over the table. The conversation made everyone a little ill at ease. The impasse was broken a few minutes later by the arrival of a high-school friend whom I had not seen for years.

This conversation contains a number of themes which repeatedly surfaced in conversations about Indians. It is important to isolate these themes and identify the subtext.

The idea that Indians have no laws is very common. It was frequently articulated by Fred and various others.

I think they're just like animals sometimes. They're always fighting or killing each other. It seems a week doesn't go by when you don't read about another one dying from alcohol or a girl being raped. You go out to the reserve, they have new houses, but the yards are full of broken cars and equipment. They don't like living in civilization. I guess it's just hard for them to obey laws and things like that. (A retired elevator employee)

I feel sorry for them. You know, they come to town and they don't know how to behave themselves. They learn, but I guess they don't have many rules out in the bush, so how would they know any better? (One of the Boys)

There are some really nice Indians and it must be hard for them because if they try to do something for themselves the rest of the tribe just takes it from them. I guess it's just every man for himself so if they like something they just take it. (A plumber)

You see the kids downtown all the time. They were never taught right from wrong so they're always getting into trouble. (One of the Boys)

The idea that Indians do not have laws or rules is consonant with the European tradition of juxtaposing white civilization, which is defined by the rule of law, to the state of savagery where there is no law. Implicit in the statement "There are no laws up there" is the notion that there are laws "down here," that is to say, in white society and, more specifically, in Thunder Bay.

Related to the image of lawless Indians is the idea that Indians do not respect possessions. In the conversation reported above, the empirical referent is the new community centre. Literally everyone I spoke to in Thunder Bay could recite an example of Indians not taking proper care of their belongings. Beaten up rusty old cars are referred to as Indian cars. The condition of houses and yards on the local reserve is a significant indicator of the Indians' supposed lack of respect for property. The Boys' theory about vandalism at the baseball diamond reflects the same idea. Stories abound of houses being torn apart by the inhabitants for firewood.

For the Boys, respectability is rooted in the notions of personal cleanliness and care of possessions. Noble poor people are clean and keep their homes or apartments neat. The extent to which they are civilized is judged by their appreciation and respect for possessions and property. Indians are thought to lack respectability and civilization and are, therefore, perceived to be different from and inferior to whites.

In the conversation described above both speakers asserted that Indians do not like whites. This idea is also very common, and it does not preclude the assumption that there are valid reasons for Indian hostility. But there is another connotation to this theme: racism is not restricted to whites. The Boys and local people in general are very sensitive to how they are stereotyped by outsiders. They sense that people who are not locals are quick to label them as racist. Thus, there is a defensiveness to their claim that Indians are just as hostile to whites as whites are to Indians.

Another theme in the conversation is that the environment can no longer support traditional Native culture. Again, the speaker has a particular example in mind but the overall notion is consistent with the long-standing image of Indian culture as dead, or at least dying. This idea has been part of white thought about Indians for centuries.

It is important to recognize that the death of the environment is attributed, in this conversation, to commercial fishermen. It is incorrect to assert, as is often done, that whites, conceived of as some homogeneous group, think of the environment as something to be conquered and used, and oppose this to the Native tradition with its belief in the importance of reciprocal relations between man and the natural world. The working class as a whole in a region such as northwestern Ontario has a very ambiguous relationship to the environment. Working-class people are dependent upon its exploitation for employment, but there is also recognition, at least among official labour organizations, that ecologically unsound management of resources is not in labour's long-term interest (Davis and Saunders 1979).[5] Moreover, nature is an important leisure resource for many people in the region. Sport fishing and hunting are popular. The environment and the practices of industry are a "hot" topic in the region. While there is a radical difference between the perception of the environment in Native cultures and economies and the way it is treated in the industrial culture and economy, it is simplistic to assume that all segments of the white population subscribe to the same view. The Boys have a strong conviction that the big corporations are environmentally irresponsible and that business is not concerned about the destruction of the natural world.

Thus, traditional Indian culture is perceived to be dying or dead, but this is seen as the outcome of commercial forces over which Indians have no control. The Boys often conceive of themselves as victims of large corporations.

Another theme in the conversation is that not all Indians are bad. At one level this can be read as a straightforward recognition of individual differences among Indians. The Boys are not dyed-in-the-wool racists with a developed theory of white superiority. As I have already stated, though, they are very sensitive about being stereotyped as such, and are quick to proclaim their innocence.

Yet there is a subtext to this assertion. It is a phrase uttered in virtually every conversation I had about Indians over two years, and the imagery in most of these conversations was negative. Statements such as "I don't hate Indians" or "I have some good friends who are Indians" or "I think Indians are all right, really" start to ring false when they are preceded or followed by a litany of negative remarks.

Another common theme is that Indians are able to live normally as long as they are in the bush. Once they leave the bush (nature) and go the reserves (civilization) they have trouble.

The most frequent complaint about Indians is that they have special privileges, that is, they receive more than their fair share of government money. In the conversation cited above, one of the speakers says that "we give them too much." The "we" in this context is the state, and, as will be shown, local whites are very critical about their relationship to the state. "We" in this context also means the taxpayer. The idea that Indians are the recipients of government largesse is the other side of the idea that no one gives the Boys anything; put another way, "we" taxpayers give but we do not receive. Sam introduced a slightly more critical version of this theme when he said, "I think it is just that we give them too much. Things they don't want. They just want to be left alone. They like how they live." The subtext in this statement is that the bureaucrats who are responsible for Indians are not aware of the real situation.

There is some ambiguity in the way the Indian is represented in the discourse of the Boys. The same can be said of the moral and ethical valuation which accompanies the different elements in the imagery. The themes of the conversation are bound up with at least six basic categories in the imagery of Indians. Each relates in some way to other elements in the local working-class culture and fixes Indians in a moral and social hierarchy.

Firstly, there is the noble savage: honest to a fault, hard working, physically tough, able to compete successfully with nature on its own terms, intelligent, and skilled in practical matters. Secondly, there is the backward simpleton: the poor sod who, try as he might, is incapable of improving himself. Thirdly, there is the Indian as victim of external forces. These three aspects of the white image of the Indian can be juxtaposed to the fourth category – the degenerate, uncivilized Indian who has no morality and is not concerned to develop it – and the fifth category – the welfare bum, lazy, shiftless, and living off other people's labour. As I have said, the Indian as welfare bum is a very important symbol today and I will discuss later its articulation with a more explicitly political discourse. Finally, there is a sixth category reserved for Indian women. On the one hand, they are degenerate. They are represented as "easy" in sexual terms. On the other hand, they are seen as victims of the degenerate Indian male. Indeed, the negative appraisal of gender relations within the Native population contributes to the image of the degenerate, uncivilized Indian male.

These six categories are assessed in ethical and social terms on the basis of their relation to other cultural values of the Boys. The noble savage is good in ethical terms and socially equal or even superior. Practical knowledge and skill, physical toughness, an ability to deal with nature, and dependability are all highly valued by the Boys. They are elements of masculinity. Dependability is particularly important because it is an aspect of the Boys' understanding of reciprocity. A good man is someone who can be relied on to contribute his share to the collective good.

The second category, the backward uncivilized savage, is morally ambiguous. It is easily related to the importance of fate in working-class culture. The uncivilized savage is to be pitied as much as disliked; fate has dealt him or her a cruel blow. However, the Boys take a paternalistic stance against a person whom they perceive as socially inferior.

The Indian as victim is a positive moral image in which the person is a social equal. This conception is arrived at on the basis of what the Indian is not – not of the power bloc, not of the dominant external forces. As I will discuss below, the distinction is central to the self-identity of the Boys and many other whites in northwestern Ontario.

The degenerate Indian is, of course, valued negatively in ethical terms and is viewed as a social inferior. Whereas the Indian as victim and Indian as backward simpleton are perceived as victims of forces over which they have no control, the degenerate Indian is seen as responsible for his or her own situation, or is thought to be too weak physically and morally to deal with his situation. The working-class men whom I know are very proud of their ability to "put up with things." They see their work as a sacrifice for the good of their family or future family. Individuals who "can't handle it" (that is, hold down a job) are scorned.

The Indian as welfare bum is a version of the degenerate-Indian theme. He or she is seen as having taken advantage of the system and, therefore, as having broken the cycle of reciprocity which is the ideal form of social exchange in the Boys' culture.

Finally, the image of Indian women constitutes them as social inferiors, consonant with the perception of all women in this culture. As easy sexual targets they are assessed negatively in terms of morality. As victims of degenerate male Indians they are viewed paternalistically.

THE INDIAN AS A SYMBOL OF THE RELATION BETWEEN THE METROPOLIS AND THE HINTERLAND

The Indian is not only an image against which local whites define themselves. It is also an important symbol in their understanding of the hinterland/metropolis relationship between the region and the centre of political and economic power in the South. Landsman (1985) has analyzed how Indians become symbols in struggles between the white population in a hinterland region and the white population in the metropolis. In upper New York state the whites perceive Indians as the subjects of media attention and the pet concern of liberal politicians located in the South. For them Indians symbolize their own alienation from the southern-based sources of political and economic power: "A major component of the interpretive framework held by Whites is the view of the Indians as a minority group, and thus as another cause of bleeding-heart downstate liberals. It was believed by Whites in both areas that the Indians were able to get what they wanted from the state in large part because they were able to dupe the downstate urban press" (Landsman 1985, 829).

This view is reflected in attitudes towards Indians expressed by whites in northwestern Ontario. The "Indian problem" is widely perceived to be the invention of whites who do not live in the region. The statement made in the conversation reported above, that "we give them too much" and that often they do not want what is given, reflects this idea.

The Indian as a symbol in the interpretation of the relationship between local whites and the southern-based power bloc was forcefully expressed in an infamous booklet produced in a town in northwestern Ontario. In the summer of 1974 the Ojibwa Warrior Society occupied Anicinabe Park in the town of Kenora. The aim of this action was to dramatize the Natives' claim to the park, and to draw attention to the deplorable condition of the Native population of the area. The reaction of many of the local whites was extremely harsh. One town resident produced a pamphlet which gained a good deal of notoriety.

The primary message of the pamphlet, tellingly entitled *Bended Elbow*, is simple and familiar. The Indians' problems stem from their own lifestyle, particularly alcohol abuse. Moreover, the government's treatment of them is too generous and lenient, which only encourages the Indians in their "slovenly" habits. The leaders of the occupation were, in the author's opinion, a few troublemakers and outsiders with connections to various international communist groups. "I don't know of any Indian living in this area who is complaining. The ones who are complaining are a few white radicals and members of the Ojibwa Warrior Society" (Jacobson 1974, 11).

The pamphlet reveals far more than the racist attitudes of its author, however. The symbolic meaning of the occupation of Anicinabe Park for the local whites can only be grasped within the context of conflicts within white society. The manner in which the government and media responded to the occupation was, for the locals, a further indication of their own alienation from the state and the South in general. The author says, "The illegal occupation goes into its fourth week, thanks to the support and encouragement of the news media given to these Indian agitators and their tactics." Moreover, "The crux of the matter is, as usual, the government. The white collar man down in Toronto or Ottawa has no idea of what goes on in the north and for that matter, doesn't seem to care" (Jacobson 1974, 12).

As in Upper New York State, the local white population maintains there is a dual system of justice and welfare. The Indians are believed to have a host of government services and benefits available to them which the whites do not, as these excerpts from the pamphlet indicate.

I ask you reader who is being discriminated against? Nobody is building me a house and furnishing it; nobody is building you a house and furnishing it. (Jacobson 1974, 6)

Education wise now an Indian boy or girl can go all the way to the top. They can be Doctors, or Nurses or anything they want to be and get paid an allowance while doing so. While the poor taxpayers can't afford to send their children to university because they have to pay the whole shot and that cost [sic] a hell of a lot. (32).

You blame the Indian Affairs for their Indian policies. Well then let's abolish

Indian Affairs. That's our tax dollars – not yours. Let's see you work for a living and to build and buy your own homes and pay for your own education. After all you don't have to accept anything from the government. I'm sure they won't mind. As to speaking out for the Indians. Why should we? Nobody speaks out for us! If we have a problem we can't even go to the "White Man's Affairs" for help – there is none. If you want equality, seriously, then cut your ties with government and their juicy grants and fine houses – step out into reality from your dream world. Pick up your load and walk with us for a mile ... The grass isn't any greener over here you know. (7)

It is asserted that the authorities do not apply the law to Indians in the same manner they do to whites. The pamphlet consists, to a large extent, of a list of what the author thinks are irresponsible and illegal habits of Indians, which the state does not prosecute. "It is a known fact that up until now, we have [sic] two sets of laws in Canada. One for the rich and one for the poor. Now there are three, because now there is a law for the Indians, which is no law at all" (Jacobson 1974, 24).

These arguments are positioned in the local culture through the author's style of thought and writing. Just as my informants, when questioned about their attitudes toward Indians, inverted the problem and posed the issue in terms of Indian attitudes about whites, on the inside front cover of *Bended Elbow* is the following statement: "The Indians refer to the taxpayer as the 'whiteman.' When in reality all taxpayers are not 'white.' So the phrase 'whiteman' in this book is Indian slang for taxpayer." Perhaps the single most important stylistic feature of the pamphlet in terms of its ability to articulate an entire cultural mode of thought is the use of the vernacular. The author defiantly proclaims her difference from those responsible for the perceived pro-Indian publicity: "The language in this article will not be nice. I believe in calling a spade a spade ... I want to tell everyone that is reading this book that I am no author. The English may even be poor" (Jacobson 1974, 1).

To employ Althusser's terminology, the fact that the article is written in the vernacular "interpellates" the reader and is the foundation of the reader's recognition of himself or herself in the author. The style is part of the system of oppositions around which the working-class culture and the sense of regionalism are constituted. The distinction between the plain language of the pamphlet and the literary language of the intellectual also reflects other dichotomies which are important in the local constitution of self-worth: the difference between mental and manual labour, common sense versus theory, the doer versus the thinker – all of these correspond to the local/outsider, northerner/southerner, and even exploited/exploiter dichotomies. Connotative linkages between these dichotomies and the situation of Natives and whites in northwestern Ontario are drawn through both the form and content of the pamphlet.

The idea that the Indians are a celebrated cause of intellectuals and other liberals from outside the region is often stated by the Boys. When it became clear that my own opinions were more sympathetic to the Native cause than their own, one of the Boys said, "Well, you've been to university and that's how you people think, but if you actually lived up here and saw what I saw, you would understand."

THE MEANING OF THE LOCAL
IMAGE OF THE INDIAN

In line with the argument that social being determines social consciousness, materialist analyses of white ideas about Indians assert that these ideas are the result of objective historical conditions. Elias (1975), in his discussion of Native-white relations in Churchill, Manitoba, sees negative white attitudes towards Natives as a reflection of the metropolis/hinterland relationship between the South and the North. Natives inhabit the northern hinterland which the southern metropolis seeks to exploit. Whites in the North represent metropolitan interests and negative white attitudes towards Native people are the manifestation and vehicle of metropolitan dominance over the hinterland.

Such an analysis is inappropriate in the present case because the local whites, at least the local white working class, are not the local representatives of metropolitan interests. They clearly perceive themselves as part of the hinterland. The feeling of alienation from the South is a fundamental feature of the identity of the whites who inhabit northwestern Ontario. According to Miller (1980, 227–8), "the feeling of belonging to an exploited hinterland is almost universal" throughout northern Ontario. Stymeist says that in Crow Lake, a town approximately three hundred kilometres northwest of Thunder Bay, southerners "are seen collectively as the exploiters of the North, as the people who take wealth out of the North but fail to improve significantly the northern standard of living" (1975, 26). The long-awaited report of the Royal Commission on the Northern Environment echoes these sentiments: "Many northerners still consider that the north has become an economic colony of the south, receiving an insufficient share of the benefits of development while bearing most of the adverse impacts. They feel that they have little control over shaping their own destinies and lack power to significantly influence decisions about development made in corporate and government boardrooms elsewhere" (Ontario 1985, 10–1).

The sense of alienation from the South is expressed in negative stereotypes northerners hold about the South. Stymeist reports that "southerners – both Canadian and American – may be regarded with a certain amount of disdain. They are seen variously as being soft, pretentious and ignorant of the land and water" (1975, 26). The Boys also hold negative images of southerners. They are perceived to be ignorant of the region's problems. Tourists and sport hunters and fishermen from the United States and southern Canada are the butt of endless jokes which revolve around the contradiction between their wealth, as expressed in the large amounts of expensive equipment they own, and their practical incompetence which prevents them from using it effectively. The fact that southern sport hunters and fishermen seem to need expensive comforts in the Bush is read as a sign that they are "soft" and unable to withstand the rigours of the climate and environment. Such ideas contain both envy and derision. Insofar as the region is relatively distant from the seat of government and is an area of resource extraction, such characterizations do reflect northerners' consciousness of the metropolis/hinterland relationship which exists between the South and the North.[6]

The South is also seen as an area torn by crime and pollution. The Boys and many others continually contrast the virtues of Thunder Bay and northwestern Ontario with the vices of the South. The South is too fast, too dirty, too crowded, too noisy, and too dangerous; the cities are too large and contain too many "weird" people. There are countless stories of people who have moved to northwestern Ontario from the southern part of the province and who "won't go back for anything," and other tales of local people who were transferred "down South" or moved voluntarily who "just can't wait to come back."

Interestingly, the romantic image of the North and its people employed by residents of northwestern Ontario to define themselves *vis-à-vis* the South is itself a southern product. It is a reflection of the frontier mythology which has been an important element in white North American culture. H.V. Nelles has summarized the image of northern Ontario in southern newspapers in the 1890s, when the government was pushing to develop its industrial frontier. "If the land was innately promising the climate would guarantee energy and intelligence required to realize that promise. For, it was commonly thought, the sharp geographical and climatic contrasts of the northern environment bred hardy, red-cheeked, self-reliant men, through whose bodies coursed a warming intelligence and vigour, and an abiding love of Anglo-Saxon liberty" (Nelles 1974, 55). Such imagery offers a metaphoric means of symbolically inverting the material relationship which exists between North and South. The North may be subordinate to the South in economic and political terms but in moral and physical terms northerners are superior to southerners.

To use Laclau's terminology (1979, 143–98) in the present historical conjuncture of northwestern Ontario, "the people"/"power bloc" distinction is expressed in terms of a North/South dichotomy. In cultural and ideological terms, the Boys' discourses based on class and those based on region are mutually reinforcing. Popular ideas condense meanings from one discourse and displace and articulate them with other discourses.

Given the strong consciousness of region among whites in northwestern Ontario, it is difficult to interpret local white attitudes toward Natives as an expression of metropolitan dominance of the region. The northern part of Ontario is an industrial frontier. The possessive individualism that often develops in an agrarian frontier has been subordinated throughout northern Ontario to a tradition of Crown ownership of the forests and minerals. In Ontario the state has always played an active role in the development of the staple products of the industrial frontier, but this did not mean it pursued socialist goals. Rather, the policies of the government reflected the concerns and needs of the southern business community.[7] The bulk of the white population was and is working class as opposed to the pattern, say, on the prairies where independent farmers settled the region.

David Stymeist (1975) has employed another kind of materialist argument to analyze relations between Natives and non-Natives in Crow Lake. He argues that white prejudice against Natives reflects the present structural position of Natives in Crow Lake and is the result of historical and contemporary structural factors. Most important is a process of informal exclusion which insures that Natives do not learn of opportunities in areas such as employment and housing. Moreover, the town has become heavily dependent on the services aimed at the impoverished Native population in the region as a source of employment. As much as a third of the employment in Crow Lake is directly related to the provision of social services for Native people. Thus, "the prejudice against Native people in Crow Lake is directly related to this economic complex, although the people of the town are not generally aware of the intricacies of the economic exchange that operates with reference to Indians ...

The creation of adverse ethnic stereotypes follows, and ethnicity, as it applies to the Native/non-Native distinction in Crow Lake, provides a logic for stratification" (Stymeist 1975, 92). In other words, ethnic prejudice represents and rationalizes the economic dominance of non-Natives over Natives.

In a region such as northwestern Ontario, however, the local white population has little control over the volume or kind of services that either the provincial or federal governments provide for Natives. These are the result of decisions made in Toronto or Ottawa. Often, the professionals who staff social service institutions are from outside the region (Stymeist 1975, 37). Weller has pointed out, for example, that "a high proportion of the local elite [throughout northwestern Ontario] is comprised [sic] of people from outside the region working for the larger companies, government, or in the professions. They often do not stay very long and do not have much identification with the region and its aspirations" (Weller 1977, 736). Moreover, whatever economic benefits accrue to the whites because of the provision of services to Native people, the whites are acutely aware that these services are paid for with their taxes. Stymeist illustrates that the white population perceives the Indians as an economic burden rather than as a source of wealth. This is evident in the Boys' own thinking and in *Bended Elbow*. Given this widespread opinion, one would expect the locals to be against the provision of social and health services to Natives. Stymeist himself states that "the people of the town are not generally aware of the intricacies of the economic exchange that operate with reference to Indians. Most whites view the position of Native people as an injustice not to the Indians but to the whites. They see their tax dollars 'supporting the Indian' and in various situations they regard this as a personal injustice" (Stymeist 1975, 92). Yet he still asserts that negative attitudes towards Natives are rooted in the fact that whites benefit from the presence of an impoverished Native population. What is required, however, is an explanation of the ideological appeal of subject categories such as the "taxpayer," and how they are articulated with some discourses rather than others. It is theoretically possible to connect the discourse about taxes to a progressive argument about the need to address the economic situation of Native people seriously, or to relate it in a positive sense to regionalism.

In the case of the Boys, and clearly in *Bended Elbow*, the negative attitudes about Indians are closely bound up with the idea that they are dependent on the welfare state. The state, it is thought, gives Indians too much. Indians are perceived to have special rights and privileges. Self-reliance and reciprocity are important values within the Boys' culture and a heavy dependence upon welfare is contrary to these values.

Moreover, there is a structural basis to the working class's low opinion of the poor.

In an indirect sense, the proletariat is exploited by all other categories with the exception of the petite bourgeoisie. Workers and the petite bourgeoisie are the only producers of all that is consumed. The surplus produced by workers is directly and indirectly (through the state) transferred as revenue to all other categories. In this sense even the poorest of the lumpenproletariat lives off the workers: given capitalist relations of production there are objective bases to the antagonism of workers to the "welfare class". (Przeworski 1986, 90)

Since Indians in northwestern Ontario comprise a large and visible part of the "welfare class" the antagonism toward the poor is transferred onto Natives as a group. The scarce resource for which whites feel they are in competition with Indians is the beneficence of the state. Competition between whites and Natives in the region is over government largesse, particularly who pays and who receives. In an ironic twist on Elias's analysis, Natives who are at the bottom of the local social hierarchy are seen by whites as having an intimate relationship with metropolitan forces from which the whites feel alienated.

Negative attitudes about Indians do not, however, only represent in ideological form a competition between whites and Natives over resources. The local discourse about Indians is also consistent with a long European tradition in which Indians are employed as a symbol in the attempt to define a moral hierarchy and, thus, to explain and justify the relations of power that exist in society at any given time. The position of a social group in these relations determines the way it uses the symbol. Indeed, struggle over the meaning of symbols is a crucial aspect of class struggle in any social formation.

Images of Indians, whether derived from the themes of the noble or depraved savage, have been employed for a variety of purposes in the struggles within European and Euro-Canadian societies. The idea of the Wild Man and Woman can be traced back to the classical thought of the Greeks and Romans, and to pre-Christian Hebrew texts. As the Middle Ages drew to a close, when Europeans discovered what they called the New World, the Wild Man/Woman had acquired characteristics, in European thought, which reflected opposing attitudes toward society and nature.

If one looked upon nature as a horrible world of struggle, as *animal* nature, and society as a condition, which for all its shortcomings, was still preferable to the natural state, then he would continue to view the Wild Man as the antitype of the *desirable humanity*, as a warning of what men would fall into if they definitively rejected society and its norms. If, on the other hand, one took his vision of nature from the cultivated countryside, from what may be called *herbal* nature, and saw society, with all its struggle, as a fall away from natural perfection, then he might be inclined to populate that nature with wild men whose function was to serve as antitypes of social existence. (White 1978, 173)

Europeans brought this cognitive map and its association of meanings with them to the New World and placed the people they encountered into this pre-existing scheme (Berkhofer 1979, 4). The myth of the Wild Man was extended into the spatial area of the New World. Images of the aboriginal people as either noble or depraved savages are examples of the same process whereby Europeans projected their own fears and desires onto others, and defined themselves against these representations. Notions of civilization, for example, were formed against ideas about savagery, it being easier to identify what civilization is not, than to give the concept a specific positive content.

For the romantics and other critics either of the absolutist state in Europe or, later, of the ravages of the industrial revolution, the Indian was a symbol of man before the Fall, physically handsome and robust, modest, dignified, brave yet tender, proud, independent, and wholesome. "According to this version, the Indian, in short, lived a life of liberty, simplicity and innocence" (Berkhofer 1979, 28). The Indian embodied what critics of the present social order imagined as the virtues of a utopian past.

In contrast to the good Indian was the image of the Indian as depraved savage. The vision is wholly negative. Warlike, naked, vain, sexually promiscuous, brutal, cowardly, dirty, lazy, treacherous, thieving, superstitious – these are the terms of the image of the bad Indian (Berkhofer 1979, 28). Such characteristics were said to typify life outside the confines of European civilization.

These attitudes were mere extensions of long-standing European ideas about civilization and savagery to the aboriginal people of the New World. The latter had no voice in the construction of these images, and their actual ways of life and cultures had relatively little impact upon the imagery. White interaction with Natives, however much bound up with material interests, was heavily influenced by these ideological structures.

White colonial policies are the result of this fear of savagery and the need to "civilize" which follows from it, as well as of crass economic interests. "Although some people may object to this claim, racism is undeniably the underlying ideology of the manifest policies regarding Native-White relations throughout the history of Canada" (Frideres 1983, 2). In some cases, this fear and desire led to the enactment of the most horrible cruelties on indigenous populations in the New World. The extermination of the Beothuck in Newfoundland, for example, cannot be explained in terms of economic factors alone since genocide was not necessary to the achievement of white domination. As Taussig suggests with respect to the horrors perpetrated against South American Indians, such phenomena represent an attempt by Europeans to exorcise the demons at the centre of their own cosmology by exterminating those onto whom those fears have been projected (1987, 3–135).

While the image of the noble savage generated more sympathetic behaviour towards Natives, the latter were still denied active participation in the construction of the imagery. The noble-savage idea became most popular in Europe after the dominance of whites in the New World was assured. Its fetishistic use was part of the attempt by the rising class of the bourgeoisie to undermine the very concept of nobility in Europe (White 1978, 191–5). Paternalism is often wrapped in a professed concern for the other, but does not necessarily involve a knowledge or acceptance of the other on his or her own terms: "In fact, what historians distinguish as high ideals and crass interests frequently combined in the past to justify specific policies, for ideals like interests derived from a larger intellectual and social context shared by the policy makers of a period or place. Moreover, what historians label good and bad motives or policies all too often produced like results for Native Americans" (Berkhofer 1979, 113–14).

The image of the noble savage was not only employed as a symbol of opposition in the criticism of Old World political regimes. It was also used as an ideal against which the lower classes within European and Euro-Canadian society could be compared.

Biological determinism, the underpinning of modern racist theory, was and is a tool of legitimation for class as well as racial and ethnic social inequality. In the absolutist state, religion provided a model which explained and justified the social hierarchy. The doctrines of liberty and equality that were central ideological features of the bourgeois revolutions created a problem for the new dominant class when those revolutions were won. Freedom and liberty for all made great political rhetoric, and helped cement the alliances of the bourgeoisie, peasants, small farmers, and workers against the aristocracy. But the freedom that was intended by the ascendant bourgeoisie was freedom from inherited aristocratic privilege, freedom of investment, and freedom to enjoy its private property. Certainly, political freedom in terms of universal suffrage and the abolition of slavery and debt bondage was not on the agenda. The political gains of the bourgeois revolutions are, of course, massively significant, but one must recognize the very limited sense in which the new dominant class wanted to apply the ideas upon which the revolutions were based (Lewontin, Rose, and Kamin 1982, 1–5).

The influence of the ideas of liberty and equality went far beyond the intentions of the bourgeoisie and it is in this context that the rise of biological determinism must be understood. By moving the argument away from the social and religious justifications for social inequality to the innate characteristics of individuals and social groups, social inequality could be explained as the result of a natural process, the product of an unalterable nature rather than social, political, and economic forces. Society could be said to be founded on principles of liberty and equality, and social inequality, exploitation, and oppression in society explained and justified at the same time (Lewontin, Rose, and Kamin 1982, 5–10).

In the nineteenth century, concomitant with the industrial revolution, the new proletariat became the object of scorn and fear to both aristocratic and bourgeois individuals. It was the "dangerous class." The new "breed" of humanity was described in racist terminology. The new industrial working population was "regarded with an alliterative hostility which betrays a response not far removed from that of the white racialist towards the coloured population today" (Thompson 1968, 207). The fear generated by this new form of human being is captured by another observer of the English industrial revolution.

As a stranger passes through the masses of human beings which have accumulated round the mills and print works ... he cannot contemplate these "crowded hives" without feelings of anxiety and apprehension almost amounting to dismay. The population, like the system to which it belongs, is NEW; but it is hourly increasing in breadth and strength. It is an aggregate of masses, our conceptions of which clothe themselves in terms that express something portentous and fearful ... as of the slow rising and gradual swelling of an ocean which must, at some future and no distant time, bear all the elements of society aloft upon its bosom, and float them Heaven knows whither. There are mighty energies slumbering in these masses ... The manufacturing population is not new in its formation alone: it is new in its habits of thought and action, which have been formed by the circumstances of its condition, with little instruction, and less guidance, from external forces. (W. Cooke Taylor 1842, cited in Thompson 1968, 208–9).

If, as Hayden White has argued, the image of the noble savage was employed in the eighteenth century by the bourgeoisie to undermine the notion of nobility so as to better criticize the aristocratic order against which it was struggling, then once that struggle was over, the notion could be employed in the ideological battle against the urban poor and the working class.

The idea that the white working class was of a lower moral order than the Indians was part of the ideology behind the reserve system. Indians had to be protected from the vices of the lower classes with whom they came into contact. On the north shore of Lake Superior and the adjacent inland regions, Indian agents were very concerned that interaction with white workers would have deleterious effects on the Natives. In the late nineteenth century, the Natives' preference for seasonal wage labour in lumber camps and on construction projects was thought by many Indian agents to account for the poor development of agriculture on the reserves and, therefore, of the civilizing effects an agricultural lifestyle was held to produce (Dunk 1987, 5). It was commonly thought that white workers set a poor example and taught "bad habits" to the Natives. As one Indian agent reported, "They are industrious and law-abiding, are never imprisoned for dishonesty, such as theft, etc., but sometimes for drinking, which is not often, as they are carefully looked after by three constables, and brought before me for trial. A great many belong to the temperance society, and never touch liquor. According to population, these Indians drink less and are better behaved than the white men by whom they are surrounded" (Canada 1897, 22). Another agent, pursuing the same theme, commented that "The Indians generally along the frontier are comparatively temperate in their habits, and especially so considering the bad example of whites around them; and I can safely say that among the same number of whites there is more drinking and a lower morality to be found than among the same number of Indians" (Canada 1890, 11).

The idea that Indians were of a higher moral character than the white working class on the frontier was not restricted to Indian agents. The use of the image of the Indian-as-noble-savage as an ideal type against which the depravity of the lower classes of Euro-Canadian society could be measured is nicely illustrated in Susanna Moodie's *Roughing It in the Bush* (1962). While quarantined in the port of Montreal in 1832 because of a cholera epidemic in the city, she describes a day's activities:

It was four o'clock when we landed on the rocks, which the rays of an intensely scorching sun had rendered so hot that I could scarcely place my foot upon them. How the people without shoes bore it I cannot imagine. Never shall I forget the extraordinary spectacle that met our sight the moment we passed the low range of bushes which formed a screen in front of the river. A crowd of many Irish immigrants had been landed during the present and former day and all this motley crew – men, women, and children, who were not confined by sickness to the sheds (which greatly resembled cattle-pens) – were employed in washing clothes or spreading them out on the rocks and bushes to dry.

The men and boys were *in* the water, while the women, with their scanty garments tucked above their knees, were tramping their bedding in tubs or holes in the rocks, which the retiring tide had left half full of water. Those who did not possess washing tubs, pails, or iron pots, or could not obtain access to a hole in the rocks, were running to and fro, screaming and scolding, in no measured terms. The confusion of Babel was among them. All talkers and no hearers – each shouting and yelling in his or her uncouth dialect, and all accompanying their vociferations with violent and extra-ordinary gestures, quite incomprehensible to the uninitiated. We were lit-erally stunned by the strife of tongues. I shrank, with feelings almost akin to fear, from the hard-featured, sunburnt women as they elbowed rudely past me.

I had heard and read much of savages, and have since seen, during my long residence in the bush, somewhat of uncivilized life, but the Indian is one of Nature's gentlemen – he never says or does a rude or vulgar thing. The vicious, uneducated barbarians, who form the surplus of overpopulous European countries, are far behind the wild man in delicacy of feeling or natural courtesy. The people who covered the island appeared perfectly destitute of shame, or even a sense of common decency. Many were almost naked, still more but partially clothed. We turned in disgust from the re-volting scene, but were unable to leave the spot until the captain had satisfied a noisy group of his own people, who were demanding a supply of stores.

And here I must observe that our passengers, who were chiefly honest Scotch labourers and mechanics from the vicinity of Edinburgh, and who while on board ship conducted themselves with the greatest propriety, and appeared the most quiet, orderly set of people in the world, no sooner set foot upon the island than they became infected by the same spirit of in-subordination and misrule, and were just as insolent and noisy as the rest. (Moodie 1962, 24–5)

The behaviour of servants towards their masters in the New World was shocking to this English lady: "The utter want of that common courtesy with which a well-brought-up European addresses the poorest of his brethren, is severely felt at first by settlers in Canada. At the period of which I am now speaking, the titles of "sir," or "madam," were very rarely applied by inferiors ... they treated our claims to their respect with marked insult and rudeness" (Moodie 1962, 139). And speaking of servants brought to Canada, she observes: "They no sooner set foot upon the Canadian shores than they become possessed with this ultra-republican spirit. All respect for their employers, all subordination is at an end; the very air of Canada severs the tie of mutual obligation which bound you together. They fancy themselves not only equal to you in rank, but that ignorance and vulgarity give them superior claims to notice" (Moodie 1962, 140). To her credit, Susanna Moodie recognized that these attitudes stemmed from the conditions of the labour market in Canada. The labouring class was not required to follow old-country traditions of deference and respect because labour was, at that time, relatively scarce in Canada.

The image of the vulgarian lower classes on the frontier is also part of contemporary culture, as represented in the stereotype of the "redneck." As I have already stated, the Boys are sensitive about outsiders' perceptions of them. Certainly, some published literary representations of the local white population have reinforced this image of local whites in northwestern Ontario. One of the better-known writers to have written of the Indians and whites in the region is Sheila Burnford, author of the best-selling animal story *The Incredible Journey* (1961). She immigrated to Port Arthur from England after the Second World War with her husband who was a physician. In 1969 she published *Without Reserve*, an account of her experiences with Native people in northwestern Ontario.

In the present context, what is of interest is how Burnford distinguishes herself from the local whites on the basis of the interests she shares with Natives. As in Moodie's account of life in nineteenth-century Canada, the Indians have certain virtues while the whites of the subordinate classes lack almost all redeeming values. This is illustrated most clearly in the following passage:

Then there was Tommy – one of three workmen on a tree-planting project of mine. One of the three was of solid Dutch stock, whose talk was mostly of a grumbling personal nature, and whose eyes brightened only at the sight of a bottle of beer; one was a gigantic Finn who said nothing at all and worked like a bulldozer – I doubt if his vision took in anything beyond the end of pick or shovel. The third was Tommy, small and slight, half Cree, half Ojib, who, as a labourer was probably not as worthy of his hire as the other two, but immeasurably worthier to me in other respects. Despite the loss of several fingers on one hand he tied strange magical flies (which he varied from day to day it seemed according to the portents) from almost anything he happened to have or pick up – a piece of fur, a feather, a rubber band or a snip of pink plastic. He could take his knife to a piece of soft wood, whittling here, slicing there, until suddenly he gently slid the slices open and there would be an intricately carved fan. And he was a mine of information to me on everything that flew, walked or swam. His hands might be digging a hole but his eyes were everywhere ...

The three were quite a study in contrasts. When they stopped for lunch and the other two had finished eating and drinking, they stretched out and had a little nap. Tommy, whose lunch had consisted of a piece of bannock fished out of his pocket and a drink of water from the lake, invariably vanished into the bush with my fishing rod and today's lethal lure. If he did not return – usually late, to the tight-lipped indignation of the other two – with a nice cleaned trout for my supper, it was always with news of something interesting going on in the bush, evidence of a bear or deer, or a hatch of partridge chicks. When it was time to down tools the others did so with promptitude, and left in the shortest possible line between (a) the site and (b) their car. Tommy was far more likely to walk around the shoreline so that he could show me where the mergansers were nesting on the way. The other two were hardworking and ambitious, and would undoubtedly get on in the New World; they were only doing odd jobs at the moment because they were temporarily laid off at one of the mills. But I always thought they only existed whereas Tommy lived. And, as though to bear this out, the trees that he put in looked far more prosperous than the others the following year. (Burnford 1969, 32–4).

The image of local whites as narrow minded can also be found in Elizabeth Kouhi's children's book *Sarah Jane of Silver Islet* (1983). The story is set in the newly constructed mining town in 1870. It revolves around, among other things, Sarah's alienation from the other local children because she enjoys books and they do not.

Tom Kelly's book *A Dream Like Mine* (1987), which recently won the Governor General's Award for fiction, is the story of a Native who kidnaps the manager of a paper mill in the vicinity of Kenora. The only local whites who appear in the book aside from manager of the paper mill and the police are three pathetic figures who are evidently petty criminals recently released from jail.

One sees, then, a two-pronged use of Indian imagery. On the one hand, there is the general practice of defining white society as a whole in either positive or negative terms against the Indian. Whites in northwestern Ontario are continuing in this long-established tradition in their negative appraisal of the Indian. On the other hand, the Indian is employed to represent an ideal against which the white working class and lower classes generally are measured and found wanting.

The Boys react against this definition of themselves. They draw attention to the actual conditions of Native people in the region, and define their own moral and intellectual worth in terms of those who are below them in the socio-economic hierarchy. Indians are a symbol of what they are not. Thus, they perceive Indians as lazy and welfare dependent and oppose this to their own self-reliance, their willingness to persevere at boring work, and their commitment to the ideal of reciprocity.

The symbolic way in which local whites define their own place in the moral universe corresponds, in this sense, to what Braroe (1975) observed in a small Prairie town:

In Short Grass the respective self-images of Indians and Whites take a dual form in which each appears morally inferior to the other. And each group acts in ways that project this image of inferiority onto the other, though largely ignorant of the result of their actions. There is a sort of negative division of symbolic labor: the attainment of a morally defensible self for both Indian and White occurs at the expense of the other, and in an atmosphere in which each represents a moral threat to the other. The failure, or refusal, of Whites to extend assistance of some kind to Indians is taken by them as evidence of their moral superiority, but is taken by the Indians as proof of White moral failure. Conversely sharing among Indians is seen by them as a reflection of their moral worth, whereas Whites see it as evidence of the Indians [sic] greediness and as a cause of their low economic and moral status. There is a complementarity in which Indians and Whites in doing what they think proper, each offer to the other clear proof of their moral deficiency. (Braroe 1975, 186–7)

Definitions of moral worth are not, however, constructed in a dichotomous relationship. For the Boys there is an important third element: the class/regional source of their own subordination. Local whites generally, and the working-class individuals who have been the specific subject of my research, do not only define themselves against the Indians. They also define themselves against the perceived dominant power bloc.

The state ideology is that Canada is a multicultural society in which ethnic differences contribute to a unique Canadian identity. Multiculturalism does not recognize the structural basis of social inequality rooted in class relations. The state's focus on ethnicity means that those who are no longer "ethnics" are assumed to be part of the "middle class" which it is imagined the vast majority of the population belongs to (McAll 1990, 165–78; Moodley 1983).

The Boys and many others in northwestern Ontario are aware that they do not belong to some mythical social group for whom class relations are unimportant. They respond to their subordination by reacting against what they perceive to be the dominant ideology of the state. They celebrate their own cultural values and vigorously reject those they feel are promoted by the power bloc. But they do so by emphasizing their own difference and superiority over the most visible ethnic group in the region. They hold their views about Indians because of a conflict over access to the resources of the state, because of a long tradition in which Indians are employed as a symbol of otherness, and because, by holding such views, they demarcate themselves from the dominant social group. For the Boys, what one thinks about Indians is a sign of what side one is on in the struggle to assert one's own moral and intellectual worth. In the Boys' ideas about Indians regionalism and ethnicity are important symbols because they relate to forms of knowledge and representation which are cultural expressions of class experience.

CHAPTER SIX

Knowledge, Work, and Hegemony

In class societies, everything takes place as if the struggle for the power to impose the legitimate mode of thought and expression that is unceasingly waged in the field of the production of symbolic goods tended to conceal, not least from the eyes of those involved in it, the contribution it makes to the delimitation of the universe of discourse, that is to say, the universe of the thinkable, and hence to the delimitation of the universe of the unthinkable.

(Bourdieu 1977, 170)

Though it is usually misrecognised, one of the things which keeps the capitalist system stable, and is one of its complex wonders, is that an important section of the subordinate class do not accept the proffered reality of the steady diminution of their own capacities. Instead they reverse the valuation of the mental/manual gradient by which they are measured.

(Willis 1977, 148)

INTRODUCTION

Common sense and anti-intellectualism are important themes in working-class culture. The negative attitudes towards women and Natives which refract the Boys' understanding of their role in the social relations of production are firmly embedded in common sense. As a mode of thought, common sense forms the substratum of the Boys' analysis of society. The Boys, and the working class as a whole, are not unique in this regard; however, common sense has a particular significance in working-class culture because of the way it relates to the subordinate position of the working class in society.

In his classic work *The Uses of Literacy*, Hoggart wrote: "If we want to capture something of the essence of working-class life ... we must say that it is 'the dense and concrete life,' a life whose main stress is the intimate, the sensory, the detailed, the personal. This would no doubt be true of working-class groups anywhere in the world" (Hoggart 1957, 104–5). The emphasis on the immediate and the concrete is a function of the dialectical process by which working-class individuals constitute their own identity. It is related to the way knowledge is defined and valued in society as a whole, and represents an inversion of the dominant ideas of what constitutes important and useful knowledge.

THE CHARACTERISTICS OF COMMON-SENSE THOUGHT

Geertz (1975b) has analyzed common sense as a systematic and totalizing form of thought, as a cultural system. It is not to be understood as an underdeveloped precursor to scientific thought but as a structured paradigm for making sense of the world. Common-sense knowledge appears natural and practical. Its ideas seem to be obvious, as if they reflect the inherent nature of whatever particular object they are directed to. It is practical in that it is defined against the impractical musings of those "whose feet aren't on the ground."[1] Moreover, there is no formal method for producing common-sense knowledge. "Commonsense wisdom is shamelessly and unapologetically ad hoc. It comes in epigrams, proverbs, obiter dicta, jokes, anecdotes, *contes morals* – a clatter of gnomic utterances – not in formal doctrines, axiomized theories or architectonic dogmas" (Geertz 1975b, 23). The absence of formality renders common-sense knowledge accessible to everyone. Its strength stems partly from the fact that it requires no special skills. However, the characteristics of common-sense knowledge are a product of a cultural system. In Geertz's words, they are qualities common sense "bestows upon things, not ones that things bestow upon it" (1975b, 22).

Bourdieu uses the concept of "doxa" to analyze common sense. Doxa are the unstated assumptions that are unstated precisely because they are perceived as obvious and natural. They contain both orthodox and heterodox opinions; they are the field within which discourse and thought take place. As he says:

Every established order tends to produce (to very different degrees and with very different means) the naturalization of its own arbitrariness. Of all the mechanisms tending to produce this effect, the most important and the best concealed is undoubtedly the dialectic of objective chances and the agents' aspirations, out which arises the *sense of limits*, commonly called the *sense of reality* ... Schemes of thought and perception can produce the objectivity that they do only by producing the misrecognition of the limits of the cognition that they do make possible, thereby founding immediate adherence in the doxic mode, to the world of tradition experienced as a "natural world" and taken for granted. (Bourdieu 1977, 164; emphasis in original)

This is very similar to the way Raymond Williams uses the notion of hegemony, which, he says, "sees the relations of domination and subordination, in their forms as practical consciousness, as in effect a saturation of the whole process of living ... to such a depth that the pressures and limits of what can ultimately be seen as a specific economic, political, and cultural system seem to most of us the pressures and limits of simple experience and common sense" (Williams 1977, 110).

In the seventeenth and eighteenth centuries common sense was celebrated as part of the opposition to the authority of Aristotle and biblical versions of reality. Common sense was an important form of thought in the move towards science and the idea that causes could be discerned through the observation of reality. Critics of aristocratic privilege and state corruption appealed to common sense.[2]

Today the term "common sense" is used in everyday speech to refer to down-to-earth thinking as opposed to theory. It connotes practical, clear-headed, simply stated solutions that are apparent to anyone, or at least anyone who is down-to-earth: "In what exactly does the merit of what is normally termed 'common sense' or 'good sense' consist? Not just in the fact that, if only implicitly, common sense applies the principle of causality, but in the much more limited fact that in a whole range of judgements common sense identifies the exact cause, simple and to hand, and does not let itself be distracted by fancy quibbles, and pseudo-profound, pseudo-scientific metaphysical mumbo-jumbo" (Gramsci in Hoare and Smith 1971, 348).

The Boys conceive of common sense in this manner. Their opinions about Indians, women, and southerners are not presented as if they are the result of long reflection and difficult analysis. In the Boys' opinion, the strength of their ideas is the fact that they are easy to arrive at; one does not need to study or reflect deeply to reach them. Their explanation of the vandalism at the baseball diamond exemplifies this attitude. When I suggested that it was possible that someone other than Indians may have been responsible, they did not understand why I needed to invent a more complex theory about the episode. Indeed, they feel that anyone who will not accept the "obvious" explanation is either emotionally weak and not able to face reality, or lacking in intelligence.

The Boys' attitude towards Indians was often couched in terms such as "It's too bad but that's the way they are." This is how our difference of opinion over the vandalism was treated. In their view I was unwilling to accept the obvious because I had been to university and had been taught, as one of them put it, that "everything should be nice." He went on to inform me that "in the real world there's a lot of shit and there's no point in pretending there isn't." In his opinion, I was being naive.

One of the Boys drew an analogy between my attitude about the vandal incident and someone from "down east" whom he had once helped when the man's car had broken down on the side of the road.

I came along and could see the hood up. It was some Japanese car, a Honda or something. I pulled up and I asked him what was the matter. He said, "I don't know, it just kind of sputtered and stopped." I asked him if he was out of gas. He said, "No, the needle said there was still gas in the tank." I said to him, "Are you sure the gas gauge works?" He said, "Sure, why wouldn't it?" So I didn't say anything for a while. He had the little book from the glove compartment out. I guess he thought it would tell him what to do. Anyway, finally I said, "Let's just try putting some gas in the tank. It can't hurt." So I got out the can I carry in the back of the van and sure enough it fires right up. I think he felt kind of stupid. He didn't even say thanks. But he's just like you. Instead of asking the obvious questions, he's digging around under the hood with that stupid book in his hand looking for some complicated problem as if he could fix it. Christ, if I hadn't shown up he probably would have started taking the plugs out and then he would have had to get a tow truck [he shook his head] ... Just use your head.

The Boys' attitudes towards women are also based upon the "obvious" facts. That women are less capable than men in most physical things is simply "true" in their opinion. It is not debatable because, according to them, anyone can see it is the case. Attempts to explain the perceived differences as the result of historical practices whereby women were denied the right to participate in these activities are viewed as efforts to complicate the issue and are ultimately thought to be irrelevant since "we live now, not yesterday." Historical explanations of Native poverty are treated in the same way. Even if they are true they are irrelevant because what is important is the present.

Common-sense thought is opposed to the forms of thought acquired through education and "book learning." The latter tends to be formalized, restricted to those who complete an educational program – and therefore élitist – abstract, and often, so it seems to many, irrelevant to practical issues. Anti-intellectualism is, for these reasons, associated with a preference for common sense.

ANTI-INTELLECTUALISM AND THE DIVISION BETWEEN MENTAL AND MANUAL LABOUR

It is necessary to define the question of anti-intellectualism in working-class culture very clearly. The statement "Anti-intellectualism is part of working-class culture" is in no way intended to suggest that working-class individuals are unintelligent, that they do not think, that they have no ideas about the world, that they are not interested in knowledge, that they are simple minded, that fundamental issues are unimportant to them, that they are more narrow minded than other social classes or groups, or that working-class individuals in any way lack the mental competence or interest possessed by other members of society. On the contrary, my argument is that anti-intellectualism is a powerful element of working-class culture precisely because workers do think, but the way they think and the things they most often have to think about are not valued by the dominant culture.

By "anti-intellectualism" I am referring to a preferred form of thought which is embedded in a set of cultural practices and beliefs, and which is formed in opposition to the perceived characteristics of other cultural practices associated with those deemed by society for various reasons to have intellectual skills. It is a way of thinking about the world and what really matters in it, a mode of approaching problems and issues that favours certain kinds of interpretations over others.

In working-class culture, common sense and anti-intellectualism are inextricably bound up with "the politico-ideological division between mental and manual labour" (Poulantzas 1978, 254) which is a dominant feature of contemporary capitalist societies. The working class's preferred form of thought is both an expression of its place on the manual side of this distinction, and a reversal of the status that the two sides have in society as a whole. Occupations on the mental side generally carry higher prestige, status, and wages than those on the manual side, yet in working-class culture the manual side is more highly valued.

The division between mental and manual labour is an ideological phenomenon based on cultural practices and rituals that separate those with a certain kind of training, those who have successfully completed a set of rituals and who therefore have credentials, from those who do not. It is not a matter of knowledge on one side and a lack of knowledge on the other. "What is involved is rather an ideological encasement of science in a whole series of rituals of knowledge, or supposed knowledge, from which the working class is excluded, and it is in this way that the mental/manual labour division functions" (Poulantzas 1978, 255). Those who perform mental labour generally possess a greater amount of "cultural capital." They have more formal education and have acquired appropriate tastes in clothing, entertainment, and food, and have learned proper forms of speech and writing; in other words, they have a certain *savoir-faire* through which they differentiate themselves from the working class.[3]

The division between mental and manual labour is not a simple social phenomenon. It is increasingly an aspect of actual labour processes. It reflects the social separation between conception and execution. This "separation of hand and brain" is one of the most significant aspects of the division of labour intensified by the capitalist mode of production, and it has significant ideological and political implications.

The novelty of this development during the past century lies not in the separate existence of hand and brain, conception and execution, but the rigor with which they are divided from one another, and then increasingly subdivided, so that conception is concentrated, insofar as possible, in ever more limited groups within management or closely associated with it. Thus, in the setting of antagonistic social relations, of alienated labor, hand and brain become not just separated, but divided and hostile and the human unity of hand and brain turns into its opposite, something less than human. (Braverman 1974, 125)

Braverman prefers the notion of the separation between conception and execution over the mental/manual labour distinction because the process of deskilling, which is, for him, an inherent feature of the capitalist mode of production, affects both sides of the dichotomy. It is necessary, according to the logic of the capitalist mode of production, because if labourers both conceive the work and execute it, it is impossible for management to enforce upon them "either the methodological efficiency or the working pace desired by capital" (Braverman 1974, 113–14). Even mental labour is divided up in this way: "Mental labor is first separated from manual labor and ... is then itself subdivided rigorously according to the same rule" (Braverman 1974, 114).

This is an important observation for it draws attention to the fact that many clerical jobs and other kinds of work in the service sector of the economy – jobs which seem to fit on the mental side of the mental/manual distinction – are as deskilled and alienating as many manual occupations. For this reason the common distinction made between blue-collar and white-collar workers is misleading. In the modern economy there are many people who do not wear blue collars to work, yet whose work involves few skills, carries little prestige, and is relatively poorly paid. Women, ethnic minorities, and youth are often the majority of workers in these categories.

The division between mental and manual labour has many implications for the experience of working-class people. What Sennett and Cobb (1973) refer to as the hidden injuries of class result from the different valuation society places on the two sides of the dichotomy. The hidden injuries are based on the low self-esteem typical of many working-class individuals, which results from the low esteem of working-class jobs and the low appreciation of working-class skills in society as a whole.

This low self-esteem produces some very painful consequences for the working class that members of other classes do not experience. Sennett and Cobb (1973, 128) provide a particularly striking example: for middle-class children, "succeeding" as defined by society at large means that they become like their parents in terms of class and culture. For working-class children, however, it means that, by definition, they must become different from their parents. Thus, working-class parents face the dilemma of either seeing their kids "fail" in the same sense they have, or of having them "succeed" but no longer having very much in common with them. Moving into the middle class means learning a different way of speaking, learning the *savoir-faire* of which Poulantzas writes, developing non-working-class interests, and it often produces a situation in which the parents do not feel comfortable in the milieu their children live in. Parents and children no longer have common interests.

The debased self-image of many working-class people is a class-based version of a colonial mentality. Many individuals internalize the middle-class visions of the working class as intellectually and culturally inferior. Working-class children who successfully make the climb into the middle class may not be truly accepted either in their new class environment or in the old. A retired elevator worker told me how during the war he was promoted to a flying officer in the Royal Canadian Air Force. When he arrived home at the end of the war, the first thing his mother did was tear his officer's stripes off his uniform to remind him that he was not "a big shot."

Sennett and Cobb's analysis poignantly illustrates some of the real pain involved in the stigma of being working class. But many working-class individuals do not passively live out the implications of the low esteem society bestows upon them. They invert the categories; they celebrate and value the manual side of the division; they delight in what educated professionals often consider mediocre mass arts and activities; they do not accept the idea that their skills, knowledge, and jobs are unimportant or of little value.

The best recent analysis of this reaction is Willis's *Learning to Labour* (1977). He follows a group of non-conformist working-class boys through the last year of school and into their first year on the job. The whole non-conformist school culture is a reaction to the formal teachings of school. It is a blatant inversion of the values the school curriculum is intended to inculcate in students. Ironically, the very rejection of the school system prepares "the lads" for the life of an unskilled labourer. They more readily fit into the shopfloor culture and are often preferred by employers over conformist students because, despite all their roughness and external disrespect for authority, their strong sense of "them" and "us" involves an implicit acceptance of "them." Students whom Willis refers to as conformists, on the other hand, accept the ideology of the system. They believe what school teaches them about the organization of society; they trust in the notion of meritocracy; they expect their work to be enjoyable and authority relations to be based on relative merit. They do not fit as easily into the shopfloor culture and are more likely to become disaffected.

Thus, the stigma of belonging to the working class, of being on the devalued side (according to the dominant ideology) of the division between mental and manual labour, does produce some psychological "injuries," but the principles upon which the manual is devalued relative to the mental are also resisted. However, resistance does not necessarily lead to a solution. Willis has shown that, ironically, this kind of resistance actually serves the needs of the system and, in the end, helps reproduce the relations upon which the mental/manual dichotomy is based.

The so-called new middle class (or new petty bourgeoisie) occupies many of the jobs which fall on the mental side of the mental/manual distinction, although this class is, of course, far from homogeneous. The growth of this class is intimately related to recent changes in the state and economy – the development of the welfare state, of monopoly capitalism, of the service sector as a major facet of the contemporary economy. The working-class reaction to the new middle class is bound together with its reaction to the welfare state, the service sector, especially publicly-funded social services, and the huge corporations, all of which are major factors in contemporary society. In northwestern Ontario the local élite is largely from outside of the region and there is a regional difference in the occupational structure (see chapter 3). The division between mental and manual labour corresponds to the split between the South and the North.

COMMON SENSE, ANTI-INTELLECTUALISM, AND THE CULTURE OF WORK

According to the Boys the manual side of this distinction is more valuable than the mental, even though this is not recognized by society as a whole, since power lies in the hands of those who perform mental labour. Within the Boys' culture it is practical knowledge and skills that are valued. The practical incompetence of intellectuals, bureaucrats, and other professionals is a fundamental conception in the cultural realm of the working class. A staple topic of conversation among my informants is the ignorance, often born of snobbery and lack of respect for the on-the-spot knowledge of the "working man," characteristic of "educated types" and management. These stories are usually performed as humorous mini-dramas. There are also many references in the local working-class idiom to this characteristic. At the grain elevator where I worked in the 1970s we had a saying for what were considered stupid ideas: we called them "jimmies," after the supervisor who, it seemed, was always inventing "more efficient" ways of doing things which usually amounted to more work for us but whose actual efficiency was highly doubtful, from our point of view.

The anti-intellectualism of the working class is a rejection of an aspect of the dominant ideology of capitalist society. As Marx outlines in the first chapter of *Capital* (1977), the capitalist mode of production gives rise to the appearance that all individuals are freely competing in the market. Success or failure appears to depend on one's achievements. For many social scientists, this is what is distinctive about modern Western society. Social status, prestige, and material wealth are the result of individual achievement rather than an ascribed location in the social hierarchy. Education is one of the means by which individuals earn these rewards. Certain kinds of knowledge have a greater exchange value than others both in terms of money capital and cultural capital.

Working-class anti-intellectualism is rooted, at one level, in an implicit critique of this ideology. It questions the assumption that some kinds of knowledge are more valuable than others, that formal education of certain kinds necessarily confers a greater use value upon one's labour. It is based on the view that the exchange value of certain kinds of knowledge and the trappings of that knowledge, such as degrees, are out of proportion to its actual use value. As Hall et al. put it, working-class anti-intellectualism

represents the response of a subordinated social class to the established hierarchical class system and the social distribution of "valid" knowledge that accompanied that hierarchy (especially as marked out educationally by certificates, examination passes, diplomas, degrees, and so on). Its anti-intellectualism is a *class* response to that unequal distribution of knowledge: a response from a class which emphasizes practical knowledge, first-hand experience of *doing things*, because it is the response of a *working class*. (Hall et al. 1978, 152; emphasis in original)

The stereotype of the professor who is pathetically incompetent at any practical activity has wide currency among the Boys. Moreover, there is a perception that occupational élites such as lawyers and doctors have a monopoly which manipulates the system to their benefit. Lawyers are categorized alongside used-car salesmen in the ethical hierarchy of occupations. They and academics are seen as contributing little to the practical needs of society.

This appraisal is based in part on old suspicions and stereotypes. It is given social force by the antagonism which develops through interactions between working-class individuals and those who hold high-status occupations. The sense of powerlessness one has when confronted with the legal system and with lawyers, the common failure of doctors to solve medical problems, the assumption that secrecy surrounds what academics actually do and why they do it – all of this reinforces the suspicion of and hostility towards élites which enjoy high social status and high incomes because of their supposed intellectual abilities.

The negative appraisal of those holding specialized knowledge also stems from experience on the shopfloor or job site. Part of this is the antagonism born of the special privileges of the technocrats and administrators – the reserved parking spots, the clean lunch rooms, the steady day shift, and the separate entrances into the office area of the plant. But it is rooted in the fact that it is working-class practical knowledge which is central to production.

Wage labour is the dominant feature of life for working-class men. It is psychologically present even when they are not physically present at their places of work. Even in its absence, it is the dominant factor in their life. The search for work, or the wait for work, becomes the dominant fact of life. Without work there is less money for living – and indeed for many working-class men this is what they work for, to really live when they are not at work. Unemployment forces people into the arms of the state bureaucracy which manages unemployment benefits. Many men and women find this humiliating. Thus, wage labour is an inescapable fact of life even when one is not at work.

The inevitability of work and the way one deals with it is of central importance in the way people like the Boys think about the social world. Work, like death and illness, is an aspect of life over which one has little control. The only rational response to this situation in their eyes is to learn to cope with it. One must suppress one's emotions and adopt an instrumental approach to the world. One of the signs that one has successfully assumed the mantle of masculinity is one's ability to deal with the world of work; to accept it as a part of life and get on with it, rather than "whining" about it. Work is fate, and one accepts fate stoically, if not happily.

The Boys are not imbued with the Protestant work ethic, at least not in Weberian terms. They do not see work as their "calling" in a religious sense. Nor do they celebrate work as a positive phenomenon in and of itself. Their attitude, in the most general sense, is simply that work is there and always will be until you retire.

Work is viewed as a kind of sacrifice – for the material goods it allows you to purchase, for the home you provide or hope to be able to provide for your wife and children. This does not mean that the Boys do not enjoy their work, or that they do not get prestige and a sense of self-worth out of the skills they learn at work. Indeed, even those involved in the most deskilled jobs can gain some positive sense of self simply from working in a place that is loud, dirty, and dangerous. Stan Gray's description of shopfloor culture in an electronics factory fits the Boys nicely.

The workingmen contrast themselves to other classes and take pride in having a concrete grasp of the physical world around them. The big shots can talk fancy and manipulate words, flout their elegance and manners. But we control the nuts and bolts of production, have our hands on the machines and gears and valves, the wires and lathes and pumps, the furnaces and spindles and batteries. We're the masters of the real and the concrete; we manipulate the steel and the lead, the wood, oil, and aluminum. What we know is genuine, the real and specific world of daily life. Workers are the wheels that make a society go round, the creators of social value and wealth. There would be no fancy society, no civilized conditions if it were not for our labour.

The male workers are contemptuous of the mild-mannered parasites and soft-spoken vultures who live off our daily sweat: the managers and directors, the judges and entertainers, the lawyers, the coupon clippers, the administrators, the insurance brokers, the legislators ... all those who profit from the shop floor, who build careers for themselves with the wealth we create. All that social overhead depends upon our mechanical skills, our concrete knowledge, our calloused hands, our technical ingenuity, our strained muscles and backs. (Gray 1987, 225–6)

Anti-intellectualism is interwoven into this cultural matrix. The Boys and all the other workers I know feel strongly that their practical experience and knowledge of the job are often ignored in both short- and long-term planning. Indeed, the poor organization of the labour process or the simple facts which are overlooked by the expert, who thus renders a work situation more difficult than it need be or a task impossible, are central themes in conversations about work.

The following three vignettes are from my field notes. They represent a kind of conversation I had many times.

I was in the bar on a Wednesday evening having a discussion about work with two men who drive pulp trucks. They were working for company A but had worked for others in the past. They were discussing which runs they preferred. One of them talked at length of how another company had a better system for loading and unloading trucks. The turn-around time was shorter than under the system company A used. "But who is going to ask us?" he said.

On another occasion, I was sitting at a kitchen table having coffee with a retired elevator worker. We were talking about building a kiln for firing pottery. Bob thought it would be a good idea to seek advice from someone at a pottery fair who has a kiln. "Maybe we could get a plan," he said. I replied that the person for whom the kiln was to be built already had a plan. "Yeah," Bob replied, "but it was made by some engineer who never used a kiln." From there Bob went on to recall larger blunders made by engineers and architects in the design of grain elevators because they "never asked the people who worked in grain elevators all their lives." He recounted how one elevator was so poorly planned that an extra two million dollars had to be spent digging a slip for ships on the opposite side to where it should have gone.[4] He mentioned how the direction of the wind was never taken into account when the elevators were built. In Thunder Bay the wind often blows off the lake and is very bitter in the winter. Bob is convinced that if the designers had ever asked the men who worked in elevators about this, much of the discomfort caused by cold and dust could have been eliminated. "Nobody ever thought or considered it important enough to ask the guy who has worked in the elevators all his life. It's just because the poor bugger in the elevator only has a grade six education."

Bob, who was a weighman, also described an elevator that had the scale-floor windows on the wrong side. They overlooked the track-shed roof so that nothing could be seen anyway. If they had been over the slip the men on the scale floor would have been able to see what was happening when they were loading a boat.

Finally, on a Saturday night I was at the home of a draftsman who has worked for a government department for thirty years. A friend and co-worker was visiting. They began to discuss work and quickly turned to a discussion of the engineers, who are their superiors on the job. The conversation revolved around which engineers were "good" and which were "bad." The deciding factor was whether or not they would consult with the local draftsmen and other less-skilled people regarding local conditions. One fellow in particular was said to be "all right" because he was "big enough" to admit when he did not know something about a particular issue and would ask the experienced subordinates on the job. He was contrasted with a newly arrived engineer from "down east" (Toronto) who never consulted the experienced local draftsmen and surveyors about anything.

The tradesmen among my informants had "a thousand stories," as one of them put it, about the poor plans produced by engineers and architects. They felt they were the ones who really knew what could and could not be done, and were continually facing situations where, if they actually followed the prescribed plans, projects could not be completed. This idea is a central feature of conversations among the Boys – how without their detailed knowledge of a process, or a piece of equipment, or a job site, nothing would get done. In his ethnography of the machine shop in Chicago, Burawoy (1979b, 46–73, 161–77) describes a similar phenomenon. The informal shopfloor culture is the basis of output restriction, but it is also the social basis for production. It is only by throwing the official instructions away and by not following the formal procedures that production goals are met. The game of "making out" is both a means by which the workers control the pace of production, and the mechanism by which they consent to the production of surplus value.

All of this indicates that there is a knowledge generated in the labour process, a practical knowledge that is essential to production but is rarely recognized by people in positions of power and authority because it is not wrapped in the cultural symbols which demarcate knowledge according to dominant definitions. Workers feel they have a special kind of knowledge based on practical experience which the experts feel can be ignored. They do not feel one needs formal training to attain this knowledge. Often, they express it in terms of its obviousness and simplicity; that is the theme in the story about the broken down car cited earlier. What is required, however, is a certain attitude – an attention to the little details that are apparent to people with a close relationship to a particular locale and activity.

The difference in approach is analogous to the difference between abstract theorizing and detailed empirical description. Indeed, this is how the difference is often expressed, though not in the same words. One interesting stylistic feature of working-class verbal communication in Thunder Bay which reflects this distinction is the way situations or scenes are reported in great detail. A conversation is recounted verbatim. Rather than summarizing the main points of a dialogue, it is re-created in the form of: "I said, then he said, then I said, then he said," and so on.

Lengthy digressions on the incompetence of the boss or foreman are another common feature of discussions of the work place. Censure is not universally applied to all supervisors for they, or at least those at the lower level, are often drawn from the ranks of the workers. Workers distinguish between "good" and "bad" foremen. But all these individuals are in an ambiguous position. On the one hand, they have personal relationships, even friendships, with the people over whom they have authority. On the other hand, they are obliged to enforce management's desires *vis-à-vis* the workers on the shopfloor. Changes in the behaviour of new foremen are closely observed by the men. Those who grow too authoritative soon become objects of ridicule. Much of the Boys humour is based on a put-down of managers and foremen.

In the track shed of the elevator where I worked the supervisor was famous for his incompetence. The track shed is where railroad cars are unloaded or loaded with grain. There are three different means of unloading. Older box cars are "shovelled" out with a board (the "shovel") which is directed by one man but pulled by cables connected to a hydraulic system. This is the oldest way of emptying a box car, and it is very dirty and physically demanding. Alternatively, box cars can be "dumped" on the "shaker," a hydraulic device which picks up the box car and literally shakes the grain into the hopper. The only manual task is sweeping the car clean after it has been emptied. The third process simply involves opening the hopper doors on the bottom of the newer tanker-style grain cars.

There are also three ways of loading grain in the track shed. The tank cars are loaded through the top. The job simply involves moving the car by means of a hydraulic winch and directing the spout to spread the grain evenly. Box cars are loaded from a spout which has to be lifted onto the grain doors which cover three-quarters of the box car's own door, then the spout must be directed to distribute grain evenly in the box car. This task is dirty because of the dust, and difficult because the spout is heavy, especially when the grain is pouring through it. The other way of loading cars involves fifty-kilogram sacks of malt piled by hand in box cars. This task is also very demanding physically.

The person who became supervisor was said to be unable to do the physically demanding jobs, so he was moved inside the elevator where the work is less arduous. But even there he was incompetent. On the transfer floor, where various kinds of grains are moved by conveyor belt from one bin to another before and after cleaning, or to the scale before loading, he apparently fell asleep in the midst of a transfer. A spill occurred and by the time it was discovered he was almost completely buried in a growing pile of grain. He was promoted to supervisor shortly after this event.

This story – I will never know if it is actually true, although the older men swore to it – took on special significance in the context of this supervisor's strict enforcement of rules perceived by the workers to be childish. He constantly complained that we talked to each other in the bagging room, where the malt was put into the sacks. He invented seemingly mindless tasks to keep the men occupied during slow periods (moving piles of grain doors from one side of the track shed to the other). The overall conviction of the men was that this was one more example of the incompetence of management in the task of organizing the labour process, and that the supervisor had been raised to this position in spite of his obvious incompetence.

The elevator superintendent's son was also employed at the elevator. He never worked in the track shed which was considered the dirtiest and hardest place to work. His father made sure he started inside the elevator and was clearly grooming him for a management position. To the men this was an indication of how the ideology of meritocracy was completely contradicted by the facts; nepotism rather than experience or skill was the important factor. We responded by ostracizing the superintendent's son; tales of his mental and physical incompetence abounded.

The negative image of the kind of knowledge exhibited by management also results from the fact that there is a great respect among workers for anyone with practical skills. Flattery often takes the form of a statement such as "Joe there, he's one hell of a nice guy, and a good electrician too." Moreover, as a group many working-class individuals are, as they say, "do-it-yourselfers." Whenever possible they avoid the market place, especially when it comes to constructing homes, refinishing interiors, making car and small equipment repairs, and so on. There is a flourishing "informal" labour exchange between individuals with different skills and different kinds of equipment. Indeed, the dominance of generalized reciprocity within the informal group is evident in this practice.[5]

These practical skills are not, however, embedded in social status differentiations, although they are an important aspect of an individual's reputation. The possession of practical skills is a necessary if not sufficient element in one's popularity. In other words, it is the demonstration of the actual use value of one's knowledge and one's skills in ways which are readily evident that counts in the assessment of an individual and of a way of thinking. The mere possession of formal training, of a degree or diploma, is not sufficient cause for respect. Thus, even though in the social formation as a whole certain kinds of knowledge and forms of thought constitute both economic and cultural capital, within working-class culture those forms are not valued culturally or economically. There is an inversion of the hierarchy. Common sense and practical skills are valued. More abstract forms of thought and less immediate and obvious skills are denigrated. They are "foreign" practices, signs of a difference. Social closure takes place around these kinds of indicators. The social displacement of the "scholarship boy or girl" is, at an individual level, an example of this. His or her success in the educational realm separates him from his former peers. There is no longer anything to discuss with his former friends and even family. There is no longer a shared language or form of thought.

WORDS AND THINGS, DOERS AND TALKERS, THEORY AND COMMON SENSE

The inversion of the division between mental and manual labour can be expressed in various other dichotomies. One is the distinction between words and things. On one side there are all those social categories and occupations in which the ability to manipulate language is the most important skill: politicians, lawyers, teachers, bureaucrats, salesmen, writers, managers, students. These people do not produce anything that is useful in the physical sense. Their value on the labour market and their social status is derived from their knowledge of a specialized language, a language designed in part at least to exclude individuals who have not performed the rituals required to gain entry into their closed world. They possess cultural capital, but not knowledge and skills that are useful in the production of things.

On the other side are the activities and occupations that involve the use of things so as to produce material objects or physical effects. These involve most of the skilled and unskilled jobs typically considered working class. Tradespeople, workers in manufacturing, transportation workers, even low-level office workers such as secretaries are considered to be people who actually do something; they do not just talk.

A retired grain-elevator worker told me once, "They have a bunker, you know, for all the politicians in case of nuclear war. They're all lawyers, those buggers. Well, they'll be sitting in the dark, because a light bulb will burn out and none of them will know what to do. They've all been to university, but they don't know their ass from a hole in the ground." This disdain for those who manipulate words rather than produce objects or perform useful services is a powerful element in the thought of the male working class in Thunder Bay.

This dichotomy is not always clear cut, however. Medical doctors, for instance, are in an ambiguous position. They are respected for their skills insofar as they operate on bodies and are able to cure physical ailments – in other words, insofar as their actions have visible material consequences – but they are not trusted because they use specialized jargon "ordinary people" do not understand and because, despite their tremendous social prestige and high incomes, their activity is often ineffectual.

The dichotomy between words and things is also expressed in the opposition of talkers and doers. In this form, it is inscribed as a dominant theme in the personal style of the Boys. Their behaviour de-emphasizes the importance of conversation in the bourgeois sense of being able to make small talk on a wide range of subjects. Being a "good conversationalist" is not a useful social skill to the Boys; it is not a skill they are concerned to develop. It has no function in their culture whereas it is very important among at least some groups in the so-called new middle class. "Networking" is a crucial aspect in the careers of many professionals. Knowing how to discuss the "in" topics and the latest intellectual fads, using an erudite turn of phrase – these are all important in the culture of professionals and intellectuals; they are aspects of the *savoir-faire* Poulantzas mentions. For the Boys they are signs of snobbery and élitism. Once, after a baseball game, I used the word "utilitarian." I was told to "fuck off with the five-dollar words and speak English."

The Boys have their own specialized languages related to their paid work and to the locale in which they live. These languages are learned in the process of everyday life; they are not the product of formal schooling. Language and styles of speech are used as boundary markers. As I described in chapter 4, foul language is used to defend the male cultural space of the pub. Technical language and slang related to work and sport are also used to define group boundaries. My argument is not that language is a symbol for some social classes and not for others, but that linguistic practices which are cultural capital within the dominant culture are seen as empty signifiers by the Boys. One's competence and worthiness is the product of one's action, not one's verbal sophistication. Given the importance in the Boys' culture of emotional control, of the ability to stoically endure discomfort and boredom, it is not surprising that they have no respect for "big" or "fast talkers" or for those, like intellectuals, for whom language usage is a game not necessarily related to any material end.

Gender stereotyping is partly based on language use: women like to talk; or, as it was sometimes put, women talk too much. Men, on the other hand, know when to be quiet. They measure their worth by what they do, not what they say.

Another dichotomy relevant to this discussion is the distinction between theory and practice. As I have already indicated, the working class is firmly on the side of practical as against theoretical knowledge. "The shopfloor abounds with apocryphal stories about the idiocy of purely theoretical knowledge. Practical ability always comes first and is a *condition* of other kinds of knowledge. Whereas in middle-class culture knowledge and qualifications are seen as a way of shifting upwards the whole mode of practical alternatives open to an individual, in working class eyes theory is riveted to particular productive practices. If it cannot earn its keep there it is to be rejected" (Willis 1977, 56; emphasis in original).

Not only is the possession of practical skills and knowledge an element in an individual's popularity but masculinity is inextricably connected to being "handy", that is, being able to repair and build things yourself. Practical skills of this nature are intrinsic to notions of manliness. They are part of the domestic division of labour within the working class. Put simply, women cook, clean, and sew; men do the large repairs to the house and car. This organization of housework is changing as greater numbers of women seek wage labour. But while men now do more tasks that were considered women's work than they did before, the time women spend in domestic labour has decreased very little if at all and the change has been resisted

(Luxton 1990a). The Boys still benefit from wives, partners, or mothers who do the bulk of the housework. The male breadwinner is still the principal role the Boys see for themselves.[6] In this division, however, female skills, while devalued, are still practical. In this sense, the division between theoretical knowledge and practical skills is perceived more as a class division than a boundary marker between genders.

Theory that produces no immediate material effects or has no obvious applicability in an actual situation is suspect. Knowledge that cannot be transformed into a practical good is a waste of time and money. From this flows a latent hostility towards university students and professors, especially those in the arts. It also has important repercussions with regard to the way the Boys perceive radical social theories. Since there is little chance that calls for radical change will amount to anything, they are perceived as useless chatter. Similarly, historical discussions of contemporary social problems are considered to be pointless since what is past is past and what matters is immediate solutions. This is illustrated in the Boys' attitudes towards Natives. Few deny Native people were mistreated and exploited historically. They feel, though, that this is irrelevant. One must learn to adjust to contemporary conditions. The past is past; one must live in the present.

THE LIMITATIONS OF ANTI-INTELLECTUALISM

The inversion of the division between mental and manual labour is, then, an oppositional practice. It is a way of marking the working class off from intellectuals and professionals, from the representatives of capital and the state. The preference for certain modes of thought is central to the identity of the Boys; it is a cultural boundary. Of course, the differences are not expressed in academic Marxist language but in terms of "the people," "the man in the street," "the regular guy" versus "the big shots," "the snobby bastards," and so on.

Categories such as these have very vague boundaries. Indeed, the petty bourgeoisie identifies quite readily with the working class on this question of the social status and economic value of experts, bureaucrats, intellectuals, and all those individuals who occupy central positions in the contemporary technocratic state. On an international scale, the resurgence of right-wing populism in the 1970s and 1980s is rooted partly in the fact that the right's attack on the welfare state is expressed in terms of the "privileged" position in society of the technocrats and bureaucrats. The failure to deal with the fact of bureaucracy either in the factory or the state as a location of class conflict is one of the reasons socialist and social democratic ideas and political parties have lost support. Right-wing ideologues have had great success linking the left with bureaucratization and the domination of everyday life by experts and technocrats.

Of course, at another level the attack on the vestiges of socialism which exist in the welfare state relies upon common sense in the way Bourdieu and Williams use the term. Leaving the economy to market forces is presented as an eminently commonsensical thing to do, since the law of supply and demand appears perfectly natural. Likewise any sensible person knows that one must live within one's means, hence it is only commonsensical that governments must cut back. Common sense indicates obvious simple solutions to problems which high-minded intellectuals and bureaucrats are too ignorant to see.

The working class is open to such ideological presentations because of its own preference for common sense as a mode of thought and the anti-intellectualism that accompanies it. This preference is a class reaction to the unequal way different kinds of knowledge are validated in society. However, it brings in its train an acceptance rather than a critique of the underlying structures of society; hence the cruel irony that a reaction to class inequality generates attitudes that actually serve to reproduce that inequality, and that a notion such as common sense, once part of the rhetoric of political radicalism, has become the means by which the status quo is preserved.

Hegemony and Resistance in Contemporary Capitalist Society

How is it possible for a cultural text which fulfills a demonstrably ideological function, as a hegemonic work whose formal categories as well as its content secure the legitimation of this or that form of class domination – how is it possible for such a text to embody a properly Utopian impulse, or to resonate a universal value inconsistent with the narrower limits of class privilege which inform its more immediate ideological vocation?

(Jameson 1981, 288)

By way of conclusion I want to draw out some of the political and theoretical implications of the preceding analysis. Although I have dealt with seemingly mundane practices and beliefs, I want to show how they, like a candle casting giant shadows, illuminate the complex and contradictory process whereby contemporary capitalist society reproduces itself.[1]

I have said that the white male working class in northwestern Ontario is quite aware of its place in the social relations of production and actively expresses resistance to its subordinate position in various symbolic ways. The Boys and the other people I spoke with are not mystified by their own lack of control over their lives as dominant ideology theories would have it. There is a common saying in Thunder Bay: "You know the golden rule; those who have the gold make the rules." The people I have discussed know they do not have the gold, and they have an idea about who does.

At the same time, however, it is evident that the Boys' understanding of their position in the social structure and their resistance to it is mediated by hegemonic cultural phenomena. It is refracted through anti-intellectualism and common-sense thought, through discourses about work and play, and ethnicity and gender, so that what originates as a perception of the way power operates in contemporary society becomes a celebration of the immediate, a willful immersion in consumption and hedonism, a negative commentary on an ethnic "other"; and throughout all of this runs a strong bias for the masculine as opposed to the feminine. Yet I have maintained that the class experience of the white male working class is crucial if one is to understand the specific meaning these other discourses have for the Boys.

My analysis runs counter to the arguments of writers such as Gorz (1982) and Laclau and Mouffe (1985), who perceive class to be just one of several subject positions through which individuals constitute their identity. I have maintained that the specific meanings non-class discourses have for white male workers can only be discerned in the light of their class experience. The Boys' existence as consumers and taxpayers is predicated on their existence as wage labourers. Other subject positions are dominated by work; for example, leisure is organized around and in opposition to work. The overwhelming priority given to common sense and the importance of anti-intellectualism is a result of working-class experience in the labour process and of the division between mental and manual labour.

This is not to suggest that non-class discourses are determined by the "economic," that they do not have a real autonomy. But meaning is always context-specific, and work is an overwhelming aspect of the context within which working-class individuals live. The meaning of non-class discourses for working-class people is inextricably bound up with this fact. As cultural "bricoleurs" they employ discourses which do not have a necessary relationship to a specific class position to interpret and express their experience. These discourses comprise the cultural tool box, and experience, which is heavily structured by one's position in the relations of production, is the "problem" to which a response must be formulated. Unfortunately, given the tools the working class have to work with, their response sometimes is ineffectual and generates further complications.

These issues are directly related to the question of how domination and subordination are reproduced in Western capitalist nations. In recent years the concept of hegemony has most frequently been used to discuss this question. It is taken from Gramsci who borrowed the term from Russian social democrats who were attempting to theorize the appropriate form of relationship between the proletariat and the peasantry in the struggle against the Tsarist state. They employed the concept of hegemony to describe the nature of an alliance between the working class and the peasants in which the former were dominant. This domination was not to be achieved by force, but through concessions and sacrifices extended by the working class to the peasantry. The hegemony of the proletariat in this alliance was conceived solely in political terms. The subjective identity of the two classes was thought to remain separate, being determined strictly at the level of the relations of production. Hegemony, according to this theory, was something apart from the subjectivity of either the working class or the peasantry (Anderson 1976, 13–16; Laclau and Mouffe 1985, 47–65).

Gramsci used the concept of hegemony inconsistently, sometimes following the meaning attributed to it by the Russian social democrats, and other times extending its terms of reference to include the idea of the cultural predominance of one class over another. In broadening the meaning of hegemony so as to include cultural as well as political dominance, Gramsci was trying to grasp the nature of bourgeois power in the Western capitalist nations. As discussed in chapter 2, according to Gramsci, in Russia the state predominated over civil society and coercion played a crucial role in the domination of the ruling class over subordinate social groups and classes. In western European nations, however, civil society was stronger and the consent of the subordinate groups and classes was a crucial aspect of bourgeois domination. This situation demanded that different revolutionary strategies be pursued. In the East, a "war of manoeuvre," an armed insurrection, was the appropriate strategy, since to capture the state was to capture society. In the West, on the other hand, a more patient game had to played; the appropriate strategy was a "war of position." The state was only an outer bulwark of society. To capture it was insufficient because the ideology of capitalism had saturated the institutions of civil society which were independent of the state. Proper cultural groundwork had to be carried out; for these ostensibly non-political institutions had to be won over to the cause of socialism before power could be taken.

In other words, the preponderance of civil society over the State in the West can be equated with the predominance of "hegemony" over "coercion" as the fundamental mode of bourgeois power in advanced capitalism. Since hegemony pertains to civil society, and civil society prevails over the State, it is the cultural ascendancy of the ruling class that essentially ensures the stability of the capitalist order. For in Gramsci's usage here, hegemony means the ideological subordination of the working class by the bourgeoisie, which enables it to rule by consent. (Anderson 1976, 24)

Anderson criticizes this formulation of the nature of hegemony because of what he deems its overemphasis on the consensual side of bourgeois domination and because it locates the site of ideological domination within civil society. For Anderson the ideological power of the bourgeoisie cannot be separated out from the nature of the state in Western capitalist nations:

The general form of the representative State – bourgeois democracy – is itself the principal ideological lynchpin of Western capitalism, whose very existence deprives the working class of the idea of socialism as *a different type of State*, and the means of communication and other mechanisms of cultural control thereafter clinch this ideological "effect." ... The political and economic orders are ... formally *separated* under capitalism. The bourgeois State thus by definition "represents" the totality of the population, *abstracted* from its distribution into social classes, as individual and equal citizens. In other words, it presents to men and women their unequal positions in civil society as if they were equal in the State. Parliament, elected every four or five years as the sovereign expression of popular will, reflects the fictive unity of the nation back to the nation as if it were their own self-government. The economic divisions within the "citizenry" are masked by the juridical parity between exploiters and exploited, and with them the complete *separation* and *non-participation* of the masses in the work of parliament. This separation is then constantly presented and represented to the masses as the ultimate incarnation of liberty: "democracy" as the terminal point of history. The existence of the parliamentary State thus constitutes the formal framework of all other ideological mechanisms of the ruling class. (Anderson 1976, 26; emphasis in original)

Thus, according to Anderson one cannot partition the ideological functions of class power in Western capitalist nations between the state and civil society. The hub of the nexus of ideological and political hegemony is the parliamentary system, although Anderson admits that cultural control plays a critical complementary role, as do market relations and the labour process (Anderson 1976, 27).

Anderson is also critical of the suggestion that coercion is not an important aspect of the exercise of class domination in the Western democracies. He argues that, rather than think in terms of coercion and consent, it is more fruitful to use the notions of domination and determination. Force is always present in the final analysis, and this is what makes it possible for consent to be generated through ideological and cultural means. We cannot deny the dominant role of culture in the Western capitalist states, but neither should we forget about the determinant role of violence. Anderson draws an analogy with the monetary system to explain what he means. The monetary system is composed of two distinct media of exchange: gold and paper. The former is never seen in actual circulation but, in its absence, it guarantees the value of the latter. In a monetary crisis everybody reverts to gold. The political system in Western capitalist nations is similar. "The normal conditions of ideological subordination of the masses – the day to day routine of parliamentary democracy – are themselves *constituted* by a silent, absent force which gives them their currency: the monopoly of legitimate violence by the State" (Anderson 1976, 41).

There are two problems with Anderson's theory of bourgeois hegemony which I wish to address. Firstly, the way that economic and political phenomena are distinguished in Western capitalist nations does, as he says, create difficulties for the perception of the actual relationship between political and economic power. However, Anderson goes too far in his depiction of the ideological function of the elected parliament and the discourses of nation and citizen. The people I have discussed are not fooled into believing that they actually exercise real power through the parliamentary system. I have shown how the sense of regionalism and the attitudes towards Native people are generated by the Boys' sense of powerlessness and by the overwhelming feeling that their votes do not make any difference. One aspect of their attitude about "Indians" involves an implicit critique of the welfare state and the bureaucracy that does not understand or seem to care about their local concerns. This, as I have also shown, is related to the inversion of the distinction between mental and manual labour, mental labour being very closely connected with the state bureaucracy. It may be true that, in general, the working-class men I have discussed do not perceive an alternative form of state to the present one, but that is different from saying that the subject position of citizen or voter overdetermines the subject position of class. They may not have an alternative, but they are not deeply committed to the present political structure. Their alienation is expressed in a deep suspicion of politics. All politicians are suspect, and politics is a corrupt game. Male workers in Thunder Bay are not unusual in this regard. According to David Halle, the workers in his American chemical plant "almost all ... view politicians as typically duplicitous and corrupt. This in their eyes is one of the most obvious truths about life in America. The people's elected representatives are a venal facade behind which real power operates" (Halle 1984, 190). It is rather strange that Marxist analysts like Anderson take the dominant ideology about how power works far more seriously than the workers do. People are less confused about how the system really operates than these commentators think.

Equally problematic is Anderson's critique of the idea that the consent of subordinate classes is the primary factor in bourgeois domination in Western capitalist nations. After his analogy between the monetary system based on paper currency and gold and the nature of consent and coercion in the Western capitalist state, he adds a proviso: "Just as gold as a material substratum of paper is a convention that needs acceptance as a media of exchange, so repression as guarantor of ideology itself depends on the assent of those who are trained to exercise it" (Anderson 1976, 42). This statement is devastating to Anderson's argument for it returns us to the beginning of the circle: which comes first, consent or coercion? How is the cultural convention regarding the legitimate use of force formed? In other words, we have returned to the question of cultural hegemony.

Anderson cannot properly address this issue because his argument is based on a simplistic idea of the relationship between the hegemony of the dominant class and the consent of a subordinate class. Hegemony does not require a conscious acceptance by the subordinate groups of the ideological vision of society put forth by the dominant class. I have argued that various discourses that contain certain ideological elements are the vehicle by which a subordinate social class expresses its opposition to the dominant social values. The ideological aspects of these discourses, however, limit their potential as a means of critically understanding the appearance of social relations.

I have maintained that class experience is crucial in understanding the significance of non-class discourses for the Boys and other people I spoke with. Yet these non-class discourses cannot be reduced simply to expressions of class. How, then, can one explain the relationship between class and non-class discourses without reducing one to the other?

Tom Nairn's (1977, 329–63) discussion of nationalism provides a useful model for understanding this relationship. Nairn castigates Marxists for not developing an adequate theory of nationalism. This is Marxism's "greatest failure." The reason for this deficiency is a preoccupation with the idea that class consciousness must predominate over other forms of consciousness. Despite the fact that workers identified themselves in terms of nationality rather than as members of a universal working class, Marxist intellectuals continued to insist that class struggle was the motor of history.

Nairn argues that nationalism has been the motivating factor in history since at least the nineteenth century. He does not, however, completely abolish class from his theory. On the contrary, class remains central to any understanding of nationalism.

There is, after all, a sense in which it is manifestly true to say that class is crucial to an understanding of nationalism. Nationalist regimentation was to a very large extent determined in its actual form and content by the class nature of the societies it affected. Their social stratification posed certain problems which it had no alternative but to solve; and the "solution" lies in the crudity, the emotionalism, the vulgar populism, the highly coloured romanticism of most nationalist ideology (all the things intellectuals have always held their noses at) ...

Nationalism could only have worked, in this sense, because it actually did provide the masses with something real and important – something that class consciousness postulated in a narrow intellectualist mode could never have furnished, a culture which however deplorable was larger, more accessible, and more relevant to mass realities than the rationalism of our Enlightenment inheritance. (Nairn 1977, 354)

Nationalism was born at the periphery of the world economic system as a reaction to the disruptions caused by colonialism and other aspects of "development." People had nothing with which to make sense of and resist the massive transformation of their lives except their culture, heritage, and language. This is why nationalism is inherently populist. While nationalism was "invented" at the periphery, it was soon adopted by the centre where real military and economic force could back up the claims of nationalist rhetoric (Nairn 1977, 336–48). What emerged as a tool of resistance against colonial domination thereby also became a weapon of colonial domination at the periphery and class domination in the metropolitan regions of the world system.

Nationalism is a specific phenomenon which cannot casually be lumped together with the issues I have analyzed. Nairn's theory of nationalism is useful in the present context, however, because he recognizes the importance of the popular practices and beliefs of people in their perception of and reaction to what is happening to them and their society. "Class consciousness postulated in a narrow intellectualist mode" (Nairn 1977, 354) cannot appeal to the subordinate classes because that narrow intellectualist mode is a form of thought characteristic of bourgeois intellectuals, a class fraction, parts of which may often be disaffected, but which remain bourgeois nonetheless.

To put it another way, one should not abandon the concept of class in favour of nationalism but, rather, understand the way nationalism, and other non-class discourses, resonate with meaning for people because of the way their class experience structures their ideas about knowledge. I have argued that the Boys' class experience gives "popular" practices and ideas a certain connotation: namely, that they belong to them, to "the people," in the struggle between the people and the power bloc. Their class experience generates a desire to embrace the local, the immediate, the obvious. Thus, it is erroneous to oppose class and nationalism or, in the present context, to oppose class to other forms of identity such as race, ethnicity, and gender. I prefer to follow Stuart Hall's advice in regard to studying racism and look at the specificities of different racisms and different systems of gender inequality. I have tried to show the logic of these systems of prejudice within the context of white male working-class culture, without simply reducing it to general ideas like competition or an inherent white racism or a male need to dominate.

Marxism as a formal political doctrine is a bourgeois intellectual product. As such, it is not, and never will be, popular among people like the Boys, at least not in its academic formal version. Given their subordinate position in society, the Boys react by celebrating what they have – their own ideas about what counts as knowledge, their own ideas about which cultural practices are important. This does limit their ability to develop a full and systematic critique of the system, but it is wrong to argue that this results from a passive acceptance of other non-class discourses. The Boys actively resist their subordination by creating another system of meaning. In this sense, they are cultural "bricoleurs," creating a meaningful universe in which they are morally and intellectually dominant.

In Western capitalist nations of the late twentieth century the impediment to the development of an explicitly anti-capitalist culture may stem from the fact that there are no longer social relations which have been untouched by commoditization, and which therefore provide a model of a real alternative. The radicalism of peasants and workers in parts of the so-called Third World is based on the fact that social systems which are relatively untouched by capitalist relations of production survive. The commoditization of life can be resisted more easily – if not more successfully – because there are still discourses derived from social activities in which use value predominates and production is organized to fulfill human needs rather than to simply produce wealth (Taussig 1980). In these societies, the state must be repressive because the memories of alternative social relations persist. In contemporary capitalist societies, the maintenance of capitalist social relations does not require extreme repression because there are no alternative discourses available. Subordinate classes and groups do not have to believe in the system or feel any particular commitment to it. They may attempt to resist it and react against it, but their cultural tool box is full of tools that were designed for other purposes by the system they are struggling against.

The process by which people like the Boys construct their own meaningful universe entails both horns of the dilemma Nairn speaks of with regard to nationalism. The cultural elements they employ are preconstrained by meanings they carry from other contexts. The Boys' use of the "Indian" to express symbolically their alienation from the southern-based power bloc reverberates with racist overtones, just as their use of lob-ball as a means of celebrating opposition to dominant cultural themes associated with the capitalist labour process is bound up with consumerism and sexism, and their celebration of common sense involves a tendency towards anti-intellectualism. The progressive impulse which lies behind the behaviours and beliefs I have discussed is blunted by the inherently regressive features of the forms of expression they chose. Like Walter Benjamin's (1968, 257–8) angel of history, the Boys move backwards into the future, intently searching through what is readily available to them for a means of making sense of the process and expressing their reaction to it. What they find, however, are cultural elements shot through with the ideological traces of other systems of domination.

Subordinate classes and groups are trapped in a veritable hall of mirrors. The commoditization of all aspects of life gives rise to appearances which mask or distort reality. In their attempt to escape this hall of mirrors and find a world where things actually are what they seem, they must use the images reflected in the mirrors. They rush to the first exit that appears only to be led into another hall of mirrors. The sole reward for their effort is, often, to become further embedded in the world they were trying to escape.

Notes

CHAPTER 1

1 See Burawoy (1979a), and Holzberg and Giovannini (1981) for reviews of the literature on industrial anthropology.

2 See Hoggart (1957, 13–18) for a perceptive discussion of romanticism in the analysis of working-class culture. Unfortunately, Hoggart himself is unable to avoid the problem.

3 "The only worker who is productive is one who produces surplus-value for the capitalist, or in other words contributes to the self-valorization of capital. If we may take an example from outside the sphere of material production, a schoolmaster is a productive worker when, in addition to belabouring the heads of his pupils, he works himself into the ground to enrich the owner of the school. That the latter has laid out his capital in a teaching factory, instead of a sausage factory, makes no difference to the relation. The concept of a productive worker therefore implies not merely a relation between the activity of work and its useful effect, between the worker and the product of his work, but also a specifically social relation of production, a relation with a historical origin which stamps the worker as capital's direct means of valorization. To be a productive worker is therefore not a piece of luck, but a misfortune" (Marx 1977, 644).

4 Burawoy shows, however, that turning the labour process into a game both gives workers some control over the pace of production, and is the means by which production takes place. In other words, while there is an element of resistance in these informal practices, the practices themselves are already incorporated into the process of producing surplus value. They are one of the means by which workers unwittingly consent to their own exploitation.

5 These figures are taken from or calculated on the basis of information in Statistics Canada (1988). They are not intended to represent a detailed, substantive statistical analysis of income and work in Thunder Bay. Rather, they are offered simply to give a rough numerical indication of how the city and the Boys as a group fit into national and provincial trends.

6 I put the term "own" in quotation marks because most working-class houses are bought with long-term mortgages. The Boys, and others in similar situations, are not likely to own their own homes outright until they are in their fifties or even sixties.

7 The fact that anthropologists refer to research done in their own society as anthropology "at home" indicates how little influence theories of social inequality have had on the discipline. Even as perceptive a writer as Marilyn Strathern (1987), who is aware that non-Western anthropologists who study their own culture cannot be said to be "at home" in the same sense that a European or North American is since anthropology is part of North American and European culture, ignores the fact of class in her discussion. She says that anthropology at home in the West is distinct from non-Western anthropologists studying their own cultures because there is a "continuity between their [the subjects of research] cultural constructs and his/hers [the anthropologist]. For they too analyse and explain their behaviour much as he/she does" (Strathern 1987, 26). The way that differences between the anthropologist and various others in his or her own society are summarily reduced or eliminated indicates a cultural blindness, which is quite inexcusable in a discipline that prides itself on its sensitivity to culture. It reflects, perhaps, the dominance in the "middle-class" professions, of which anthropology is one, of the liberal ideology that "we are all middle class now." It is surely correct to argue that for a Malaysian to undertake anthropology at home is not the same thing as for an English man or woman (or Canadian) to do anthropology at home. However, to argue that all members of Western society explain their own world in much the same way as the anthropologist does is to ignore all the significant, if sometimes subtle, differences in terms of economics, politics, and culture which are an essential aspect of Western capitalist societies. However much anthropological ideas are part of a broad Western cultural heritage, anthropology is a discursive arena peculiar to members of the professional middle classes or those aspiring to that position. Anthropology was not invented by the working class, but by bourgeois gentlemen far removed from material needs. Its ideas and language are not part of the everyday world in which the working class lives.

8 Boot hockey is essentially the same as normal ice hockey except skates are not worn.

9 "Bourgeois respondents particularly distinguish themselves by their ability to control the survey situation (and any analysis of survey data should take this into account). Control over the social situation in which culture operates is given to them by the very unequally distributed capacity to adopt the relation to language which is called for in all situations of polite conversation" (Bourdieu 1984, 174).

10 The notion of structured totality comes from Althusser (1977), especially the essay entitled "Contradiction and Overdetermination." For a useful discussion of the difference between a structured and expressive totality in the context of debates about work and working-class ideology and politics, see Burawoy (1985, 54–63).

11 For a presentation of the female voice see Luxton (1980).

12 Throughout the book the terms Native, Native people, Amerindian, aboriginal people, and indigenous people refer to the actual first inhabitants of the continent. Indian denotes the stereotypes and images of Natives which are part of European and Euro-Canadian culture in the past and present.

CHAPTER 2

1 Gramsci was not consistent in his use of the term civil society (Anderson 1976). It can be understood, however, as a concept which designates an intermediate area between the economy and the state. It is the area of social institutions commonly referred to as private. "It is the sphere of 'private' interests in general" (Hall, Lumley and McLennan 1977, 47).

2 In the Althusserian scheme, ideology refers to one of the three instances that comprise social existence. It includes both the formalized political discourses and the entire realm of meaning. It thus includes what I call culture. I maintain a distinction between culture and ideology, using the second of these terms only in reference to the explicit and formalized discourses with an explicit political and moral intent.

3 For a discussion of "bricolage" and subcultural style see Clarke (1976).

4 "It can be persuasively argued that all or nearly all initiatives and contributions, even when they take on manifestly alternative or oppositional forms, are in practice tied to the hegemonic: that the dominant culture, so to say, at once produces and limits its own forms of counter-culture" (Williams 1977, 114).

5 Laclau employs Althusserian terminology and thus does not distinguish between culture and ideology.

6 A recent example of this is Davis's (1980) discussion of the American working class. His whole analysis is based on the question of why the American working class did not follow the "normal" path of development.

7 "Penetration" is an unfortunate term in that it can be read as having patriarchal undertones. Except where I directly quote Willis, I employ the term "perception." In the quote which follows, perception could replace penetration and the meaning of the passage would not be altered.

8 Part of the Laclau/Mouffe argument is that production should not be viewed as a purely economic phenomenon. Theories such as Braverman's (1974), which argue that the tendency towards deskilling is an economic requirement of capitalism and that it is proletarianizing an ever greater number of workers and, therefore, generating an ever larger number of alienated individuals who are potentially class-conscious (socialist) workers are seen as examples of this economism. Laclau and Mouffe argue that there are no laws of capitalist development which simply unfold; rather, there is a struggle in the production process and the nature of any labour process is a result of this struggle rather than of immutable laws of development. I agree with this point, as well as with the idea that the workers' place in the production process does not necessarily generate a consciousness that embodies or resembles Marxist or socialist theory. But it is wrong to suggest that the experience of the production process is not a massive presence in the lives of workers and that it does not have a very heavy influence on the consciousness of working-class individuals. One's position in production relations is not merely one subject position among many, since many others ultimately depend on it, and others such as sex, ethnicity, and race are reinterpreted in light of the experience of production. Indeed, by relegating production relations to simply one of several subject positions in opposition to those who see it as the determinant of consciousness as a whole, Laclau and Mouffe are guilty of what Geras refers to as either/or argumentation: that is, arguing either that everything is determined at the economic level, or that nothing is; there is no room for a middle ground. See Geras (1987) and the reply by Laclau and Mouffe (1987). Also, for a critique of Braverman's critics see Sheila Cohen (1987).

9 Goldmann distinguishes *conscience réelle* and *conscience possible*. The former is what people actually think, while the latter is a limiting concept to cover ideas and values which are necessary to the existence of the group itself. The real consciousness may contain many other ideas, but the possible consciousness describes ideas that must be there. In the examples I refer to, he says in their real consciousness many of

the peasants may actually want to migrate to the city, but as long as they remain small proprietors they have to believe in private property. Goldman is, of course, following Lukacs. There is a subtle but important difference, however, between the suggestion that a structural position in economic terms entails certain interests, without specifying in what form those interests will be expressed, and the argument that a structural position does or should entail a specific form of consciousness with regard to society as a whole.

CHAPTER 3

1 There are various spellings of Kaministikwia.
2 The historian J.M.S. Careless has aptly remarked, "Successive opulent suburbs of Toronto spell out a veritable progression of northern mining booms" (in Nelles 1974, 118–19). In the case of Silver Islet, however, the owners were based in New York City and Detroit.
3 Hereafter TBEDC.
4 The national average is 5.0 per cent and the provincial average is 4.0 per cent. At the time of writing there is serious concern over the future of the port. The drought on the prairies and the federal government's desire to ship more grain out of the West Coast are threatening the port. It is projected that as many as fifteen hundred jobs related to the storage and shipment of grain may be lost unless the federal government alters its current policy which favours West Coast ports.
5 Quetico Centre. 1977. *Priorities for Action*. A corporate study cited in Lakehead Social Planning Council (1981, 1).
6 Formerly Great Lakes Forest Products.
7 For a discussion of "structures of feeling" see Williams (1977, 128–35). Williams's definition is necessarily complex given that he is trying to describe a process rather than things.

The term is difficult, but "feeling" is chosen to emphasize a distinction from the more formal concepts of "world-view" or "ideology." It is not only that we must go beyond formally held and systematic beliefs, though of course we have always to include them. It is that we are concerned with meanings and values as they are actively lived and felt, and the relations between these and formal or systematic beliefs are in practice variable (including historically variable), over a range of from formal assent with private dissent to the more nuanced interaction between selected and interpreted beliefs and acted and justified experiences ... We are talking about characteristic elements of impulse, restraint, and tone; specifically affective elements of consciousness and relationships:

not feeling against thought, but thought as felt and feeling as thought: practical consciousness of a present kind, in a living and interrelating continuity. (Williams 1977, 132)

8 The regional division of mental and manual labour is probably greater than these rough figures indicate. Many Native reserves and communities in northwestern Ontario are incompletely enumerated. Undoubtedly the figures for people employed in primary occupations would be higher for northwestern Ontario if these communities were included, given the importance of hunting, trapping, fishing, and seasonal work in other primary industries for many Native communities. Secondly, the categories used by Statistics Canada do not reveal the actual level of control and responsibility exercised by individuals working in the managerial and administrative category, or in the technological, social, religious, artistic, and clerical occupations. The relative absence of the senior government and corporate executives from the region means that, often, people in management and administration or in the technological and social science professions are themselves overseeing the implementation of plans formulated by people in head office or the ministerial offices. Therefore, the figures I have used under-represent the actual extent to which the division between mental and manual labour corresponds to a division between northwestern Ontario and the southern metropolitan region.

9 "The willingness of the workmen of the staple trades to accept the conditions of their employments without much complaint is not easily explicable in terms of pecuniary calculation. Indeed, although these men were paid money for their work and did many things that industrial men do, their behaviour was largely the product of considerations beyond the measures of economic rationality. They were as disciplined in their way as industrial men, but theirs was an extroverted discipline distinct from the cold, methodical routine of factories. They invented but had no cult of invention. They were efficient, not from devotion to a religion of capitalism but as a matter of personal pride. They resisted retrogression, but they did not know that man must progress. Their choice of occupation was determined primarily by local custom. The values that kept them to it were familiarity and excitement. They acquired prestige by exhibitions, not of accumulation, but of strength and daring. The pattern of their lives displays an extreme discounting of the future for which the rational foundation, if there was one, must have been that life in any case is short" (Pentland 1981, 178).

10 During the two years I was in Thunder Bay (June 1984 to August 1986) the hourly wage rates in these types of jobs ranged from ten to fifteen dollars.

11 Admittedly, the census data for Indian reserves is not reliable. None-theless, the figures do give a general indication of the magnitude of the differences.

12 Armstrong and Armstrong (1984) is the classic study of the economic situation of women in Canada.

13 Percentages are calculated from figures in Statistics Canada (1988). They have been rounded off.

14 This figure applies to full-year/full-time workers. For part-year/part-time work women earn forty-eight per cent of what men do.

15 This statement is based on calculations using figures in Statistics Canada (1988). Specifically, female part-year/part-time workers as a percentage of all female workers are 66.5 per cent in Rainy River District, 66.3 per cent in Kenora District, 63.9 per cent in Thunder Bay District, 55.3 per cent in Ontario, and 58.2 per cent in Canada.

CHAPTER 4

1 This is the goal of the "human relations school" of industrial relations.

2 The dichotomy between the freedom of leisure time and the control over behaviour at work is not unique to capitalist society. It is a feature of the life of the working class in modern socialist societies and was a characteristic of modes of production based on slavery, as, for example, in the southern United States before 1865.

3 British football hooligans have received much attention in recent years. But spectator violence is not exclusive to the British – it has even been reported in the Soviet Union – and is not a particularly recent development: the Montreal hockey riot took place in 1955. In 1970, Honduras and El Salvador fought the famous "football war" (Taylor 1982, 40–1).

4 At the time of writing the league described below is still going strong and some of the Boys are still playing, which means these individuals have been playing for close to a decade.

5 The presence of what the Boys perceive to be a significant Native clientele is one such symbol. The classification of people in ethnic terms is very much based upon common-sense stereotypes, so that there may in fact be a clientele of people of Native ancestry at the bars frequented by the Boys, but unless they fulfill the Boys' image of what Indians look like they are not recognized.

Other significant symbols are such things as dress codes, plants, wall decorations, the type of music played, and so on. As I argue throughout the text, the social environment the Boys live in is pregnant with meaning, and they are acute observers of what many classify as insignificant or mediocre phenomena. A sign in a doorway which reads "No jeans or baseball uniforms" speaks volumes to the Boys about

what sort of clientele the bar wants to cater to, and what kind of people frequent such a place.

6 The same can be said of 1990.

7 This refers to the situation in 1986. The number of teams and some
of the sponsors have changed since then.

8 These are 1986 prices.

9 The description that follows is from 28 June 1984. I was not a member of the team at this point. The events described are representative
of many evenings of lob-ball that I observed and participated in.

10 This is a pseudonym. Personal names have been changed throughout
the book.

11 My doubts about whether I could characterize the bar as working
class were allayed months later when the wife of a psychology professor at the local university informed me that if I really wanted to know
what the working class is like I should go to this bar. She had been
there once, she said, shaking her head and raising her eyebrows.

12 The tournament described here took place 14–16 June 1985. I was a
member of the team at this point.

13 The characters of this television comedy include three hillbilly brothers, two of whom are named Daryl.

14 The benefit raised almost $4,000.

15 The trip discussed here took place over the July Fourth weekend,
1985. The tournament was part of the Independence Day celebrations in the United States.

16 Despite their active pursuit of a good time, the Boys were very responsible with regard to drinking and driving. As I have said, wives
or girlfriends were often designated drivers, but if they were not in
attendance, someone took it easy, or taxis were used. The carnivalesque atmosphere rarely degrades into what might be considered socially irresponsible actions. As with carnival everywhere, there are
recognized temporal and spatial limits which the women especially try
to enforce.

17 Morton (1982) argues that, despite Soviet claims to the contrary, sport
in the Soviet Union has in some ways developed similarly to sport in
Western capitalist nations. It places an "exaggerated emphasis" on
élite sports and suffers from overcommercialization.

18 This aspect of local sports history has not been investigated; however,
it is part of the popular history of the area. Many older individuals
reported the practice to me and could name people who were employed by companies but whose actual main duty was to play baseball
or hockey for the company team.

19 Violence in hockey at all levels of play is a major concern of sports
officials in Canada. The federal government established a "Commis-

sion on Fair Play" in 1986. One of the Boys' major criticisms of "Hockey Night in Canada" telecasts is that they do not show replays of fights.

20 One team had a member with a crippled leg which prevented him from running. He played back-catcher for them, a position which required relatively little mobility, and he took a regular turn at bat and ran the bases as best he could.

21 This amounted to no more than creating lineups for each game. The Boys asked him to do this because they felt there were too many arguments among themselves about what positions they would play. Aside from this, though, the "coach" was not an authority figure.

22 At the time he was working in a factory in Fort William in which aircraft were built. Today the same plant is owned by a subsidiary of Lavalin Corporation and produces rapid-transit cars for subways.

23 On the melancholy of Western Marxism and the role of humour in Marxist cultural theory see the discussion in Eagleton (1985, 143–72).

24 The Boys in my study were young and their relationships with their girlfriends and wives were, with a couple of exceptions, still in the courting stage; that is, children and lack of money had not yet come between them, and their roles as parents had not overshadowed their relationships as lovers (Rubin 1976, 49–68). This was equally true of couples who lived together and those who did not.

25 Only one of these relationships survived. The man in this case returned to the local community college and upon graduation found a job in his line of work in Toronto. The woman, who had a professional degree from a university and was working in her profession in Thunder Bay, followed him.

CHAPTER 5

1 I use both "racial" and "ethnic" here on purpose. In the past, there was apparently some discussion of the biological differences between different Europeans, and, of course, the term race was not used in a manner consistent with modern anthropological definitions. A newspaper article on sanitation conditions in the Italian section of Fort William in 1909 begins with the following question: "Have you ever wondered why many of the Latin races of southern Europe and South America are never free from plague, the ravages of which kill more people yearly than earthquakes and wars combined?" (*Daily Times-Journal* 21 August 1909, 1). For the rest of this section I will follow the recent convention and refer simply to ethnicity.

2 The entire elevator and malt plant employed approximately one hundred people.

3 "At one end of the scale are the 'core' ethnics, people who possess and act out the cultural stuff of their origins a fair percentage of the time. Most core ethnics are older people. Next there are the 'peripheral' ethnics, those who may be familiar with the language and customs of an ethnic category, but seldom if ever use them. This is the archetypal second generation. Finally, there are the 'name' ethnics, people who are regarded as having an ethnic dimension simply because their ancestors are or are assumed to have been 'ethnics'" (Stymeist 1975, 54).

The brief analysis presented here does not imply that ethnicity no longer matters to people. There are active and popular voluntary associations in Thunder Bay based upon ethnicity. However, ethnicity among European immigrants and their descendants does not provide the logic of social inequality in the city and region.

4 "The notion of ideology appears to me to be difficult to make use of for three reasons. The first is that like it or not, it always stands in virtual opposition to something else which is supposed to count as truth. Now I believe that the problem does not consist in drawing the line between that in a discourse which falls under the category of scientificity, or truth, and that which comes under some other category, but in seeing historically how effects of truth are produced within discourses which in themselves are neither true nor false" (Foucault 1980, 118).

5 For another critical review of the forest industry out of Thunder Bay see Lakehead Social Planning Council (1981).

6 See Weller (1977) for an application of the hinterland/metropolis model to the politics of northwestern Ontario.

7 This thesis is further developed in Nelles (1974, 426–88).

CHAPTER 6

1 This statement is from my own notes. It is one of the many sayings through which the mental/manual distinction is expressed. On numerous occasions they were used to describe me, since it often seemed I was incapable of grasping what was obvious to everyone else.

2 Thomas Paine, the English radical, titled one of his most influential pamphlets *Common Sense* (1791).

3 The relationship between cultural and economic capital, and domination and subordination is the main subject in Bourdieu (1984).

4 I do not know if this story is true. What is important in the present context is what it reveals about Bob's attitude towards professionals such as architects and engineers.

5 This is true of families as well. Lending equipment, cars, or trucks, and giving advice is very common. The classic working-class community may be gone, but with the automobile and telephones the extended family as an economic unit persists, albeit in an altered form. One does not have to live with parents and siblings to see them frequently and to maintain mutual dependence and obligations.

6 Even the stereotype of the male breadwinner is apparently changing among some groups of industrial workers. The impetus for this among the steelworkers studied by Livingstone and Luxton (1989) was a union-sponsored drive to hire women. None of the Boys' places of work had such a program.

CONCLUSION

1 The imagery is suggested by a passage in Taussig (1982, 3).

Bibliography

Adorno, T.W., and Max Horkheimer. 1979. *Dialectic of Enlightenment*. London: Verso.

Aguilar, John L. 1981. Insider Research: An Ethnography of a Debate. In *Anthropologists at Home in North America: Methods and Issues in the Study of One's Own Society*. Ed. Donald A. Messerschmidt. New York: Cambridge University Press, 15–26.

Althusser, Louis. 1971. Ideology and Ideological State Apparatuses. In *Lenin and Philosophy and Other Essays*. London: Verso.

– 1977. *For Marx*. London: Verso.

Anderson, Benedict. 1984. *Imagined Communities: Reflections on the Origin and Spread of Nationalism*. London: Verso.

Anderson, Perry. 1976. The Antinomies of Antonio Gramsci. *New Left Review* 100:3–73.

Arens, W. 1981. Professional Football: An American Symbol and Ritual. In *The American Dimension: Cultural Myths and Social Realities*. Ed. S. Montague and W. Arens. Sherman Oaks, California: Alfred Publishing, 3–14.

Armstrong, Pat, and Hugh Armstrong. 1984. *The Double Ghetto: Canadian Women and Their Segregated Work*. 2d ed. Toronto: McClelland and Stewart.

Arthur, Elizabeth. 1968. The Landing and the Plot. *Lakehead University Review* 1:1–17.

– 1986. An Outpost of the Empire: The Martin Fall Post of the Hudson's Bay Company, 1821–78. *Ontario History* 78(1):5–23.

Arthur, Elizabeth, ed. 1973. *Thunder Bay District 1821–1892: A Collection of Documents*. Toronto: The Champlain Society.

Baker, William J. 1979. The Making of a Working-Class Football Culture in Victorian England. *Journal of Social History* 13:241–52.

Bakhtin, Mikhail. 1984. *Rabelais and His World*. Bloomington: Indiana University Press.

Barr, Elinor. 1988. *Silver Islet: Striking It Rich in Lake Superior*. Toronto: Natural Heritage/Natural History Inc.

Barr, Elinor, and Betty Dyck. 1979. *Ignace: A Saga of the Shield*. Winnipeg: Prairie Publishing Corporation.

Barthes, Roland. 1973. *Mythologies*. London: Granada.

Belmonte, Thomas. 1979. *The Broken Fountain*. New York: Columbia University Press.

Benjamin, Walter. 1968. *Illuminations*. Ed. Hannah Arendt. New York: Harcourt, Brace and World.

Berkhofer, Robert F. 1979. *The Whiteman's Indian: Images of the American Indian from Columbus to the Present*. New York: Vintage.

Birrell, Susan. 1981. Sport as Ritual: Interpretations from Durkheim to Goffman. *Social Forces* 60:354–76.

Bishop, Charles. 1974. *The Northern Ojibwa and the Fur Trade: An Historical and Ecological Study*. Toronto: Holt, Rinehart and Winston.

Blue, Archibald. 1896. The Story of Silver Islet. In *Sixth Report of the Ontario Bureau of Mines*. Toronto: Warwick Brothers.

Bourdieu, Pierre. 1977. *Outline of a Theory of Practice*. London: Cambridge University Press.

– 1984. *Distinction: A Social Critique of the Judgement of Taste*. Cambridge, Massachusetts: Harvard University Press.

Brantlinger, Patrick. 1990. *Crusoe's Footprints: Cultural Studies in Britain and America*. New York and London: Routledge.

Braroe, Niels Winther. 1975. *Indian and White: Self Image and Interaction in a Canadian Plains Community*. Stanford: Stanford University Press.

Braverman, H. 1974. *Labor and Monopoly Capital: The Degradation of Work in the Twentieth Century*. New York: Monthly Review Press.

Burawoy, Michael. 1979a. The Anthropology of Industrial Work. *Annual Review of Anthropology* 8:231–66.

– 1979b. *Manufacturing Consent: Changes in the Labor Process Under Monopoly Capitalism*. Chicago: University of Chicago Press.

– 1985. *The Politics of Production: Factory Regimes Under Capitalism and Socialism*. London: Verso.

Burnford, Sheila. 1961. *The Incredible Journey*. Boston: Little, Brown.

– 1969. *Without Reserve*. London: Hodder and Stoughton.

Campbell, Susan. 1980. *Fort William: Living and Working at the Post*. Thunder Bay: Old Fort William and Ontario Ministry of Culture and Recreation.

Canada. 1890. *Sessional Papers* no. 12. "Department of Indian Affairs Annual Report." Ottawa: Queen's Printer.

– 1897. *Sessional Papers* no. 14. "Department of Indian Affairs Annual Report." Ottawa: Queen's Printer.

Carrigan, Tim, Bob Connell, and John Lee. 1987. Hard and Heavy: Toward a New Sociology of Masculinity. In *Beyond Patriarchy: Essays by Men on*

Pleasure, Power and Change. Ed. Michael Kaufman. Toronto: Oxford University Press, 139–92.

Chute, Janet E. 1986. A Century of Native Leadership: Shingwaukonse and His Heirs. Ph.D. thesis, McMaster University.

Clarke, John. 1976. Style. In *Resistance Through Rituals: Youth Subcultures in Post-War Britain*. Ed. Stuart Hall and Tony Jefferson. London: Hutchison, 175–91.

– 1979. Capital and Culture: The Post-War Working Class Revisited. In *Working Class Culture: Studies in History and Theory*. Ed. John Clarke, Chas Critcher, and Richard Johnson. London: Hutchison, 238–53.

Clarke, John, and Chas Critcher. 1985. *The Devil Makes Work: Leisure in Capitalist Britain*. Urbana and Chicago: University of Illinois Press.

Clarke, John, Chas Critcher, and Richard Johnson, eds. 1979. *Working Class Culture: Studies in History and Theory*. London: Hutchison.

Clifford, James. 1988. *The Predicament of Culture: Twentieth-Century Ethnography, Literature, and Art*. Cambridge, Massachusetts: Harvard University Press.

Clifford, James, and George Marcus, eds. 1986. *Writing Culture: The Poetics and Politics of Ethnography*. Berkeley: University of California Press.

Cohen, Sheila. 1987. A Labour Process to Nowhere? *New Left Review* 165:34–50.

Crawford, Robert. 1984. A Cultural Account of "Health": Control, Release, and the Social Body. In *Issues in the Political Economy of Health Care*. Ed. John B. McKinley. New York: Tavistock, 60–103.

Critcher, Chas. 1979. Football Since the War. In *Working Class Culture: Studies in History and Theory*. Ed. John Clarke, Chas Critcher, and Richard Johnson. London: Hutchison, 161–84.

Davis, Mike. 1980. Why the US Working Class is Different. *New Left Review* 123:3–44.

Davis, Ron, and Graham Saunders. 1979. *Unions North of 50*. Prepared for the Thunder Bay and District Labour Council. Submitted to the Royal Commission on the Northern Environment.

Dawson, Ken. 1983. *Prehistory of Northern Ontario*. Thunder Bay: Thunder Bay Historical Museum Society.

Dominion Bureau of Statistics. 1913. *Fifth Census of Canada 1911, Volume II. Religions, Origins, Birthplace, Citizenship, Literacy and Infirmities, by Provinces, Districts and Subdistricts*. Ottawa: H.C. Parmalee, Printer to the King's Most Excellent Majesty.

– 1936. *Seventh Census of Canada 1931, Volume 1. Summary*. Ottawa: J.O. Patenaude, ISO, Printer to the King's Most Excellent Majesty.

Donnelly, Peter. 1988. Sport as a Site for Popular Resistance. In *Popular Cultures and Political Practices*. Ed. Richard B. Gruneau. Toronto: Garamond Press, 11–32.

Driben, Paul, and Robert S. Trudeau. 1983. *When Freedom is Lost: The Dark Side of the Relationship between Government and the Fort Hope Band.* Toronto: University of Toronto Press.

Dunk, Thomas W. 1987. Indian Participation in the Industrial Economy on the North Shore of Lake Superior, 1869–1940. *Thunder Bay Historical Museum Society Papers and Records* 15:3–13.

Dunning, R.W. 1959. *Social and Economic Change Among the Northern Ojibwa.* Toronto: University of Toronto Press.

Eagleton, Terry. 1985. *Walter Benjamin or Towards a Revolutionary Criticism.* London: Verso.

Easterbrook, W.T., and H.G.J. Aitken. 1980. *Canadian Economic History.* Toronto: Gage.

Eklund, William. 1981. The Formative Years of the Finnish Organization of Canada. In *Finnish Diaspora 1: Canada, South America, Africa, Australia and Sweden.* Ed. Michael G. Harney. Toronto: Multicultural History Society of Ontario, 49–60.

Elias, Peter. 1975. *Metropolis and Hinterland in Northern Manitoba.* Winnipeg: Manitoba Museum of Man and Nature.

Engels, F. [1845] 1969. *The Condition of the Working Class in England.* London: Granada.

Foucault, Michel. 1980. Truth and Power. In *Power/Knowledge: Selected Interviews and Other Writings 1972–1977 by Michel Foucault.* Ed. Colin Gordon. New York: Pantheon, 109–33.

Frideres, James S. 1983. *Native People in Canada: Contemporary Conflicts.* 2d ed. Scarborough: Prentice-Hall.

Geertz, Clifford. 1975a. Deep Play: Notes on the Balinese Cockfight. In *The Interpretation of Cultures.* New York: Basic Books, 412–53.

– 1975b. Common Sense as a Cultural System. *The Antioch Review* 33(1):5–26.

Geras, Norman. 1987. Post-Marxism? *New Left Review* 163:40–82.

Godelier, Maurice. 1978. Infrastructures, Societies and History. *Current Anthropology* 19(4):763–71.

Goldmann, Lucien. 1970. Conscience Réelle et Conscience Possible, Conscience Adéquate et Fausse Conscience. In *Marxisme et Sciences Humaines.* Paris: Gallimard, 121–9.

Gorz, A. 1982. *Farewell to the Working Class: An Essay on Post-Industrial Socialism.* London: Pluto Press.

Gray, Stan. 1987. Sharing the Shop Floor. In *Beyond Patriarchy: Essays by Men on Pleasure, Power, and Change.* Ed. Michael Kaufman. Toronto: Oxford University Press, 216–34.

Hall, John. 1980. Ethnic Tensions and Economics: Indian-White Interaction in a British Columbia Ranching Community. *Canadian Journal of Anthropology* 1(2):179–90.

Hall, Stuart. 1980. Race, Articulation and Societies Structured in Dominance. In UNESCO. *Sociological Theories: Race and Colonialism*. Paris: UNESCO, 305–45.

Hall, Stuart, and Tony Jefferson, eds. 1976. *Resistance Through Rituals: Youth Subcultures in Post-War Britain*. London: Hutchison.

Hall, Stuart, Bob Lumley, and Gregor McLennan. 1977. Politics and Ideology: Gramsci. In *On Ideology*. Centre for Contemporary Cultural Studies. London: Hutchison.

Hall, Stuart et al. 1978. *Policing the Crisis: Mugging, the State, and Law and Order*. London: Macmillan Press.

Halle, David. 1984. *America's Working Man: Work, Home, and Politics Among Blue-Collar Property Owners*. Chicago and London: The University of Chicago Press.

Hargreaves, John. 1982. Sport and Hegemony: Some Theoretical Problems. In *Sport, Culture and the Modern State*. Ed. Hart Cantelon and Richard Gruneau. Toronto: University of Toronto Press, 141–97.

Hebdige, Dick. 1979. *Subculture: The Meaning of Style*. London and New York: Methuen.

Hey, Valerie. 1986. *Patriarchy and Pub Culture*. London and New York: Tavistock.

Hickerson, Harold. 1970. *The Chippewa and Their Neighbours: A Study in Ethnohistory*. New York: Holt, Rinehart and Winston.

Hoare, Quintin, and Geoffrey Nowell Smith, eds. 1971. *Selections from the Prison Notebooks of Antonio Gramsci*. New York: International Publishers.

Hoch, Paul. 1972. *Rip Off the Big Game: The Exploitation of Sports by the Power Elite*. Garden City, NY: Anchor Books.

Hoggart, Richard. 1957. *The Uses of Literacy*. London: Chatto and Windus.

Holzberg, Carol S., and Maureen J. Giovannini. 1981. Anthropology and Industry: Reappraisal and New Directions. *Annual Review of Anthropology* 10:317–60.

Jacobs, Jerry. 1984. *The Mall: An Attempted Escape from Everyday Life*. Prospect Heights: Waveland Press.

Jacobson, Eleanor. 1974. *Bended Elbow: Kenora Ontario Talks Back*. Kenora: Central Publications.

Jameson, Fredric. 1981. *The Political Unconscious: Narrative as a Socially Symbolic Act*. Ithaca: Cornell University Press.

Johnson, Richard. 1979. Three Problematics: Elements of a Theory of Working-Class Culture. In *Working Class Culture: Studies in History and Theory*. Ed. J. Clarke, C. Critcher, and R. Johnson. London: Hutchison, 201–37.

Kelly, M.T. 1987. *A Dream Like Mine*. Toronto: Stoddart Publishing Co. Limited.

Komarovsky, Mirra. 1967. *Blue-Collar Marriage*. New York: Vintage.

Korr, Charles P. 1978. West Ham United Football Club and the Beginnings of Professional Football in East London. *Journal of Contemporary History* 13:211–32.

Kouhi, Elizabeth. 1983. *Sarah Jane of Silver Islet*. Winnipeg: Queenston House Publishing Co. Ltd.

Kue Young, T. 1987. The Health of Indians in Northwestern Ontario: A Historical Perspective. In *Health and Canadian Society: Sociological Perspectives*. 2d ed. Ed. David Coburn et al. Markham: Fitzhenry and Whiteside, 109–26.

Laclau, E. 1979. *Politics and Ideology in Marxist Theory*. London: Verso.

Laclau, E., and C. Mouffe. 1985. *Hegemony and Socialist Strategy: Towards a Radical Democratic Politics*. London: Verso.

– 1987. Post-Marxism Without Apologies. *New Left Review* 166:79–106.

Lakehead Social Planning Council. 1980. *Thunder Bay: A Socio-Economic Study from a Social Planning Perspective*. Thunder Bay: Lakehead Social Planning Council.

– 1981. *The Forest Industry in Northwestern Ontario: A Socio-Economic Study from a Social Planning Perspective*. Thunder Bay: Lakehead Social Planning Council.

– 1983. *Target Population Profile: Natives. Community Needs Priorization Project*. Thunder Bay: Lakehead Social Planning Council.

Landsman, Gail. 1985. Ganienkeh: Symbol and Politics in an Indian/White Conflict. *American Anthropologist* 87(4):826–39.

Leach, E.R. 1967. Caste, Class and Slavery: the Taxonomic Problem. In *Caste and Race*. Ed. A. de Reuck and J. Knight. London: Ciba Foundation, 5–16.

Lévi-Strauss, Claude. 1966. *The Savage Mind*. London: Weidenfeld and Nicolson.

Lewontin, Richard, Steven Rose, and Leo Kamin. 1982. Bourgeois Ideology and the Origins of Biological Determinism. *Race and Class* 24(1):1–16.

Livingstone, D.W., and Meg Luxton. 1989. Gender Consciousness at Work: Modification of the Male Breadwinner Norm Among Steelworkers and their Spouses. *The Canadian Review of Sociology and Anthropology* 26(2):240–75.

Lukacs, Georg. 1971. *History and Class Consciousness*. Translated by Rodney Livingstone. London: Merlin.

Luxton, Meg. 1980. *More Than a Labour of Love*. Toronto: The Women's Press.

– 1990a. Two Hands for the Clock: Changing Patterns in the Gendered Division of Labour in the Home. In *Through the Kitchen Window: The Politics of Home and Family*. Ed. Meg Luxton, Harriet Rosenberg, and Sedef Arat-Koc. Toronto: Garamond Press, 39–55.

– 1990b. From Ladies' Auxiliaries to Wives' Committees: Housewives and the Unions. In *Through the Kitchen Window: The Politics of Home and Family*.

Ed. Meg Luxton, Harriet Rosenberg, and Sedef Arat-Koc. Toronto: Garamond Press, 105–21.

McAll, Christopher. 1990. *Class, Ethnicity, and Social Inequality*. Montreal: McGill-Queen's University Press.

MacDonald, Marvin. 1976. An Examination of Protestant Reaction Toward the non-English-speaking Immigrant in Port Arthur and Fort William, 1903–1914. MA thesis, Lakehead University.

Mann, Michael. 1973. *Consciousness and Action Among the Western Working Class*. London: Macmillan.

Marcus, George. 1986. Contemporary Problems of Ethnography in the Modern World System. In *Writing Culture: The Poetics and Politics of Ethnography*. Ed. James Clifford and George Marcus. Berkeley: University of California Press, 165–93.

Marx, Karl. [1867] 1977. *Capital, Volume 1*. New York: Vintage.

– [1852] 1978. *The Eighteenth Brumaire of Louis Bonaparte*. Peking: Foreign Languages Press.

Marx, K., and F. Engels. [1848] 1968. *The Communist Manifesto*. New York: Modern Reader Paperbacks.

Miller, Tom. 1980. Cabin-Fever: The Province of Ontario and Its Norths. In *Government and Politics of Ontario*. 2d ed. Ed. Donald MacDonald. Toronto: Van Nostrand Rheinhold, 227–44.

Moodie, Susanna. [1854] 1962. *Roughing it in the Bush*. Toronto: McClelland and Stewart.

Moodley, Kogila. 1983. Canadian Multiculturalism as Ideology. *Ethnic and Racial Studies* 6:320–31.

Morrison, Jean. 1974. Community and Conflict: A Study of the Canadian Working Class and Its Relationships at the Canadian Lakehead, 1903–1913. MA thesis, Lakehead University.

– 1976. Ethnicity and Violence: The Lakehead Freighthandlers Before World War 1. In *Essays in Canadian Working Class History*. Ed. Gregory S. Kealey and Peter Warrian. Toronto: McLelland and Stewart, 143–60.

Morton, Henry. 1982. Soviet Sport Reassessed. In *Sport, Culture and the Modern State*. Ed. Hart Cantelon and Richard Gruneau. Toronto: University of Toronto Press, 209–19.

Nairn, Tom. 1973. The English Working Class. In *Ideology in Social Science*. Ed. Robin Blackburn. New York: Vintage Books, 187–206.

– 1977. *The Break-Up of Britain: Crisis and Neo-Nationalism*. London: New Left Books.

Native People of Thunder Bay Development Corporation. 1983. *Shattered Dreams: An Employment and Related Needs Study of Native Women in Thunder Bay*. N.p.

Nelles, H.V. 1974. *The Politics of Development: Forests, Mines, and Hydro-Electric Power in Ontario, 1849–1941*. Toronto: Macmillan.

Ontario. Ministry of the Attorney General. 1985. *Royal Commission on the*

Northern Environment: Final Report and Recommendations. Toronto: Ontario Ministry of the Attorney General.

Ontario. Ministry of Tourism and Recreation. N.d. *Northwestern Ontario Sports Database Study: Executive Summary.* Toronto: Ontario Ministry of Tourism and Recreation.

Paine, Thomas. 1791. *Common Sense: Addressed to the Inhabitants of America.* Philadelphia: W. and T. Bradford.

Palmer, Bryan D. 1979. *A Culture in Conflict.* Montreal: McGill-Queen's University Press.

Pentland, H. Clare. 1981. *Labour and Capital in Canada 1650–1860.* Toronto: James Lorimer and Company.

Pilli, Arjo. 1981. Finnish-Canadian Radicalism and the Government of Canada from the First World War to the Depression. In *Finnish Diaspora 1: Canada, South America, Africa, Australia and Sweden.* Ed. Michael G. Harney. Toronto: Multicultural History Society of Ontario, 19–32.

Poulantzas, Nicos. 1978. *Classes in Contemporary Capitalism.* London: Verso.

Przeworski, Adam. 1986. *Capitalism and Social Democracy.* Cambridge: Cambridge University Press.

Pucci, Antonio. 1978. A Community in the Making: A Case Study of a Benevolent Society in Fort William's "Little Italy." *Thunder Bay Historical Museum Society Papers and Records* 6:16–27.

Rader, B.G. 1979. Modern Sports: In Search of Interpretations. *Journal of Social History* 13:307–21.

Radforth, Ian. 1981. Finnish Lumber Workers in Ontario, 1919–1946. *Polyphony* 3(2):23–34.

– 1987. *Bushworkers and Bosses: Logging in Northern Ontario 1900–1980.* Toronto: University of Toronto Press.

Rasporich, A.W. 1973. A Boston Yankee in Prince Arthur's Landing: C.D. Howe and His Constituency. *Canada: An Historical Magazine* 1:21–40.

– 1974. Factionalism and Class in Modern Lakehead Politics. *Lakehead University Review* 7:31–65.

Ray, Arthur J. 1974. *Indians in the Fur Trade: Their Role as Trappers, Hunters and Middlemen in the Lands Southwest of Hudson Bay, 1660–1870.* Toronto: University of Toronto Press.

Reiss, S.A. 1980. Sport and the American Dream: A Review Essay. *Journal of Social History* 14:295–303.

Robinson, William. N.d. Report of William Robinson to Colonel Bruce, Superintendant General of Indian Affairs. Toronto. 24 September 1850. NAC, RG10, Vol. 191, Document 5451, Microfilm Reel No. 11,513.

Rousseau, J. 1978. Classe et ethnicité. *Anthropologie et Sociétiés* 2(1):61–9.

Rubin, Lillian Breslow. 1976. *Worlds of Pain: Life in the Working Class Family.* New York: Basic Books.

Sahlins, Marshall. 1972. *Stone Age Economics*. New York: Aldine.

Saul, John. 1979. The Dialectic of Class and Tribe. *Race and Class* 20:347–72.

Schleppi, John R. 1979. It Pays: John H. Patterson and Industrial Recreation at the National Cash Register Company. *Journal of Sport History* 6:20–8.

Scott, Don. 1975. Northern Alienation. In *Government and Politics of Ontario*. Ed. Donald MacDonald. Toronto: Macmillan, 235–48.

Sennett, R., and J. Cobb. 1973. *The Hidden Injuries of Class*. New York: Vintage.

Shivji, I. 1976. *Class Struggles in Tanzania*. New York: Monthly Review Press.

Shkilnyk, Anastasia. 1985. *A Poison Stronger Than Love: The Destruction of an Ojibwa Community*. New Haven: Yale University Press.

Sider, Gerald. 1986. *Culture and Class in Anthropology and History: A Newfoundland Illustration*. Cambridge and Paris: Cambridge University Press and Editions de la Maison des Sciences de l'Homme.

Siggner, Andrew J. 1986. The Socio-Demographic Conditions of Registered Indians. In *Arduous Journey: Canadian Indians and Decolonization*. Ed. J. Rick Ponting. Toronto: McClelland and Stewart, 57–83.

Spindler, George, and Louise Spindler. 1983. Anthropologists View American Culture. *Annual Review of Anthropology* 12:49–78.

Statistics Canada. 1973. *1971 Census of Canada*. Volume 1, Part 1. Catalogue 92–702. Ottawa: Minister of Supply and Services.

– 1982. *1981 Census of Canada: Population – Geographic Distributions, Ontario*. Catalogue 93–906. Ottawa: Minister of Supply and Services.

– 1988. *Census Canada 1986: Profiles Ontario, Part 2*. Catalogue No. 94–112. Ottawa: Ministry of Supply and Services.

Stedman Jones, Gareth. 1983. Rethinking Chartism. In *Languages of Class*. London: Cambridge University Press, 90–178.

Stewart, Bryce M. 1913a. Report of a Preliminary and General Social Survey of Fort William, March 1913. Directed by the Department of Temperance and Moral Reform of the Methodist Church and the Department of Social Service and Evangelism of the Presbyterian Church. N.p.

– 1913b. Report of a Preliminary and General Social Survey of Port Arthur, March 1913. Directed by the Department of Temperance and Moral Reform of the Methodist Church and the Department of Social Service and Evangelism of the Presbyterian Church. N.p.

Strathern, Marilyn. 1987. The Limits of Auto-Anthropology. In *Anthropology at Home*. Ed. Michael Jackson. ASA Monograph 25. London: Tavistock, 16–37.

Stymeist, David. 1975. *Ethnics and Indians: Social Relations in a Northwestern Ontario Town*. Toronto: Peter Martin Associates Limited.

Taussig, Michael. 1980. *The Devil and Commodity Fetishism in South America*. Chapel Hill: The University of North Carolina Press.

– 1982. *Coming Home: Ritual and Labour Migration in a Columbian Town.* Montreal: Centre for Developing Area Studies, Working Paper Series No. 30.

– 1987. *Shamanism, Colonialism and the Wild Man: A Study in Terror and Healing.* Chicago: University of Chicago Press.

Taylor, Ian. 1982. Class, Violence and Sport: The Case of Soccer Hooliganism in Britain. In *Sport, Culture, and the Modern State.* Ed. Hart Cantelon and Richard Gruneau. Toronto: University of Toronto Press, 39–96.

Thompson, E.P. 1968. *The Making of the English Working Class.* Harmondsworth: Penguin.

– 1978a. Folklore, Anthropology and Social History. *Indian Historical Review* 3(3):247–66.

– 1978b. Eighteenth-Century English Society: Class Struggle Without Class? *Social History* 3(2):133–65.

– 1978c. *The Poverty of Theory.* New York: Monthly Review Press.

Thunder Bay, City of. 1985. *Population and Labour Force Projection Update 1981–2001.* Thunder Bay. N.p.

Thunder Bay Economic Development Corporation. 1988. *Thunder Bay Factbook.* Thunder Bay: Thunder Bay Economic Development Corporation.

Tolvanen, Ahti. 1981. Finns in Port Arthur in the Interwar Period: A Perspective on Urban Integration. In *Finnish Diaspora 1: Canada, South America, Africa, Australia and Sweden.* Ed. Michael G. Karney. Toronto: Multicultural History Society of Ontario, 61–76.

Trigger, Bruce. 1986. The Historians' Indian: Native Americans in Canadian Historical Writing from Charlevoix to the Present. *Canadian Historical Review* 67(3):315–42.

Troyer, Warner. 1977. *No Safe Place.* Toronto: Clarke, Irwin.

Turnbull, Colin. 1968. The Importance of Flux in Two Hunting Societies. In *Man the Hunter.* Ed. R.B. Lee and Irven Devore. Chicago: Aldine, 132–7.

Weber, Max. 1958. *The Protestant Ethic and the Spirit of Capitalism.* New York: Charles Scribner's Sons.

Weller, Geoffrey. 1977. Hinterland Politics: The Case of Northwestern Ontario. *Canadian Journal of Political Science* 10(4):727–54.

– 1980. Resource Development in Northern Ontario: A Case Study in Hinterland Politics. In *Resources and the Environment: Policy Perspectives for Canada.* Ed. O.P. Dwivedi. Toronto: McClelland and Stewart, 243–68.

– 1986. Health Care Delivery in the Canadian North: The Case of Northwestern Ontario. Paper presented at the annual meeting of the Western Association of Sociology and Anthropology, Thunder Bay, 13–15 February 1986.

Wheeler, Robert F. 1978. Organized Sport and Organized Labour: The Workers' Sports Movement. *Journal of Contemporary History* 13:191–210.

White, Hayden. 1978. *Tropics of Discourse: Essays in Cultural Criticism*. Baltimore: Johns Hopkins University Press.

Williams, G. 1973. *Simpson's Letters to London 1841–1842*. London: The Hudson's Bay Record Society.

Williams, Raymond. 1963. *Culture and Society 1780–1950*. Harmondsworth: Penguin.

– 1977. *Marxism and Literature*. Oxford: Oxford University Press.

Willis, Paul. 1977. *Learning to Labour: How Working Class Kids Get Working Class Jobs*. Farnsworth: Saxon House.

– 1979. Shop-floor Culture, Masculinity and the Wage Form. In *Working Class Culture: Studies in History and Theory*. Ed. John Clarke, Chas Critcher, and Richard Johnson. London: Hutchison, 185–98.

Wright, Erik Olin. 1976. Class Boundaries in Advanced Capitalist Societies. *New Left Review* 98:3–41.

Young, Michael, and Peter Willmott. 1962. *Family and Kinship in East London*. Rev. ed. New York: Penguin.

Index